Breaking Free

The Empath's 10-Step Guide to Surviving Toxic Relationships With Narcissists

Published by Peter Sanglass

Peter Sanglass

Contents

Preface

When I first found myself in a narcissistic relationship, I didn't understand the depth of what I was getting into. I had always been a deeply sensitive, emotionally attuned person. I felt everything intensely, from the joy of others' successes to the weight of their pain. In many ways, I thought my empathy was my greatest gift, the very thing that made me connect so deeply with people and care so profoundly. But it was also the very thing that became my undoing in the hands of someone who lacked empathy altogether.

Looking back, I can see now that my marriage wasn't just toxic—it was emotionally abusive, and I was caught in a cycle that drained me until I barely recognized myself. My self-worth was entangled with my partner's needs, and my emotional energy was constantly siphoned away, leaving me depleted, confused, and disconnected from my own truth. It wasn't until I broke free from that relationship that I was able to piece together the lessons I had learned —the lessons that became the foundation of

Breaking Free: The Empath's 10-Step Guide to Surviving Toxic Relationships With Narcissists.

In the beginning, I had no idea what narcissism was. I didn't know how it could destroy someone's sense of self or leave a person feeling unworthy of their own emotions. All I knew was that my life had become a whirlwind of confusion, guilt, and emotional turbulence. I questioned myself constantly: *Is it me? Am I being unreasonable? Why do I feel so drained and emotionally raw?* These were the questions that plagued me every day. And when I finally learned the truth—that I had been living with a narcissist—I felt both relief and shame. Relief, because I finally understood that I wasn't crazy, that the emotional chaos I had endured was a pattern, not a series of random events. But also shame, because I felt I should have known better, that my sensitivity had somehow made me an easy target for manipulation.

But this is where the journey began. I realized that my sensitivity and empathy weren't weaknesses— they were part of who I was, and they had a profound power when harnessed correctly. The problem wasn't my empathy. The problem was how I had allowed it to be exploited. What I came to understand over time, and what I now share with you through this book, is that empaths are deeply vulnerable in a world that is often narcissistic and emotionally exploitative. Narcissists are drawn to the energy and emotional openness of empaths because we care deeply, we nurture without question, and we try to fix what's broken. These traits make us prime candidates for manipulation.

What I learned, however, is that our capacity for compassion and care doesn't have to come at the expense of ourselves. It doesn't have to mean losing ourselves to the needs and demands of others, especially those who don't have our best interests at heart. The journey to becoming an empowered empath is about recognizing our worth, setting healthy boundaries, and embracing our sensitivity as a source of strength rather than something to be exploited.

The first step in my own transformation was learning to recognize the signs of a toxic relationship. Narcissism, emotional manipulation, and gaslighting were all foreign concepts to me at the time, but once I understood them, the fog started to lift. I began to see the patterns—the constant devaluation, the emotional rollercoaster, the love-bombing followed by cruelty, and the incessant gaslighting that made me doubt my own reality. The hardest part of this realization was understanding that I didn't have to endure this. I didn't have to keep trying to "fix" a person who wasn't interested in healing. I was allowed to protect myself, to stand up for my needs, and to say no.

And that's where the real work began.

I had to learn how to set boundaries—boundaries that felt foreign and uncomfortable at first, but that became essential as I began to reclaim my sense of self. As an empath, saying "no" felt like a betrayal. I had been taught that love meant giving endlessly and sacrificing myself for the happiness of others. But I quickly realized that without boundaries, I would never be able to protect my own emotional space, and I would continue to be preyed upon by narcissistic individuals.

Through this book, I share the tools that helped me navigate the challenge of building healthy boundaries: how to assert myself without guilt, how to recognize the difference between selflessness and self-sacrifice, and how to communicate my needs calmly and firmly. This was not just about saying "no" to others—it was about learning to say "yes" to myself.

But healing isn't just about learning boundaries. It's also about reclaiming your self-worth. After years of emotional neglect and manipulation, I had forgotten what it felt like to believe in my own value. The process of rebuilding self-esteem was painful but essential. It required deep self-compassion and the willingness to let go of the toxic beliefs I had internalized over the years—beliefs that I wasn't enough, that I had to earn love, and that my worth was tied to the approval of others.

Part of the healing process was reconnecting with myself, rediscovering the passions and interests that had been buried under the weight of my marriage. I began to honor the things that brought me joy, whether it was writing, painting, or spending time in nature. I learned that joy wasn't a luxury—it was necessary for my emotional and physical well-being. When we live authentically, we create space for the things that nourish us, and that in turn, empowers us to face the challenges ahead.

I also learned the importance of seeking professional help. For too long, I had believed that I could handle everything on my own, that I could "fix" the relationship, that if I just loved harder or tried more, things would get better. It wasn't until I sought therapy that I realized how deeply wounded I had been and how much I needed to heal. Therapy, especially trauma-informed therapy, was an essential part of my recovery. It helped me process the emotional wounds that had been inflicted over years, helped me understand the dynamics of narcissistic abuse, and most importantly, it gave me the tools to move forward.

Through this book, I share the therapeutic tools that helped me reclaim my emotional well-being, from cognitive-behavioral techniques to mindfulness and self-compassion practices. These tools are designed to help you move past self-blame, rebuild your self-esteem, and begin healing from the wounds that have been inflicted upon you. I want you to know that you are not alone in this journey, and that healing is not only possible but probable, when you take the necessary steps to protect and nurture yourself.

The most profound lesson I learned on this journey is that being an empath is not a curse; it's a gift. But it's a gift that needs to be protected, nurtured, and used wisely. We empaths have the capacity to change the world with our empathy, but only if we first take care of ourselves. I learned that my sensitivity, when tempered with wisdom and healthy boundaries, could become my greatest source of strength. I learned to stand in my power, not to shut down my empathy, but to wield it intentionally—to give without overextending, to care without losing myself, and to love without compromising my sense of self.

I wrote this book to share my story, to help others who may feel lost or trapped in relationships that drain them, to show them that there is a way out. I want you to know that there is hope for you, just as there was hope for me. You can break free from the patterns of manipulation and emotional abuse, and you can reclaim your life, your joy, and your power.

The journey isn't easy, but it is worth it. You are worth it.

Empathy is not a weakness—it is your superpower. When you learn to harness it with strength, wisdom, and compassion, you can create the life you were always meant to live. I hope that this book serves as a guide, a light in the darkness, and a reminder that no matter what you've been through, you are capable of thriving.

Take the first step today. Reclaim your power.

Introduction

Being an empath is an extraordinary gift. Empaths possess an innate ability to feel the emotions of others deeply, sometimes as if those emotions were their own. This heightened sensitivity can lead to profound connections with others, a deep understanding of people, and an almost supernatural capacity for compassion. But, as with any powerful gift, there is a price to pay. For empaths, that price often comes in the form of vulnerability—particularly in a world that is increasingly narcissistic, self-centered, and emotionally disconnected.

The truth is, being an empath in today's society can feel like a double-edged sword. On one hand, empaths offer a depth of empathy and understanding that the world desperately needs. On the other, they are often left feeling overwhelmed, drained, and vulnerable to the toxic energy of narcissistic individuals. Navigating relationships in such an environment can be an emotionally taxing experience that, if left unchecked, can lead to feelings of hopelessness, confusion, and self-doubt.

In *Breaking Free: The Empath's 10-Step Guide to Surviving Toxic Relationships With Narcissists*, we embark on a transformative journey—a journey from vulnerability to empowerment. This guide is designed for empaths who find themselves trapped in toxic relationships, whether with narcissistic partners, friends, family members, or coworkers. Over the course of ten steps, we will explore practical strategies for empaths to protect their emotional well-being, set healthy boundaries, and reclaim their power. Through this guide, empaths will learn not only how to survive toxic dynamics, but how to thrive beyond them.

What Does It Mean to Be an Empath?

At the heart of being an empath is the ability to deeply sense and absorb the emotions of others. This heightened empathy goes beyond mere sympathy—it is the ability to feel the joy, sadness, pain, or anger of someone else as though those emotions are one's own. It is a profound, often involuntary, connection to the emotional states of those around you.

Empaths are often highly intuitive, able to read subtle emotional cues such as body language, facial expressions, and unspoken feelings. They might sense when someone is lying, when someone is in emotional distress, or when a situation feels "off," even without a clear explanation. This sensitivity allows empaths to connect with others on a deep and meaningful level. They often find fulfillment in helping others, offering comfort, and providing a safe space for others to express themselves.

However, being an empath is not without its challenges. The very traits that make empaths such loving and supportive individuals can also leave them vulnerable to emotional burnout. An empath's ability to absorb the energy around them, while a gift, can also become overwhelming. The more time an empath spends around emotionally charged individuals or in toxic environments, the more likely they are to internalize those emotions, which can result in physical and emotional exhaustion, anxiety, and even depression.

The Challenges Empaths Face in a Narcissistic World

To understand the difficulties empaths face, it is crucial to explore the environment they navigate—a world that has, unfortunately, become increasingly narcissistic. Narcissism, at its core, involves an excessive preoccupation with oneself, a lack of empathy for others, and an insatiable need for admiration. In relationships with narcissists, empaths are often subjected to manipulation, emotional exploitation, and emotional neglect.

Narcissistic individuals are masters of emotional control. They thrive on creating imbalances in relationships, often using tactics such as gaslighting, guilt-tripping, and emotional withdrawal to maintain their dominance. Empaths, with their natural tendency to absorb the emotions of others, are particularly vulnerable to these tactics. Narcissists often exploit the empath's empathy, using their emotional sensitivity as a means to control, manipulate, or drain them.

In many ways, the empath and the narcissist form a toxic, symbiotic relationship. The empath seeks to nurture and heal, while the narcissist feeds off their emotional energy, leaving the empath emotionally depleted and confused. Over time, this dynamic can lead to significant emotional damage. The empath may feel as though they are constantly giving, but never receiving, leading to a loss of self-worth and identity.

Moreover, the narcissistic world in which empaths live is often a world that values power, success, and control above compassion and vulnerability. The "me first" mentality of modern society can leave empaths feeling isolated and misunderstood. The empathy that comes so naturally to them is often viewed as a weakness, or worse, something to be exploited. This leaves empaths with a deep sense of loneliness and frustration as they struggle to find connections that nourish them emotionally and spiritually.

For empaths, the world can feel like a battleground of emotional manipulation and exploitation. They may feel overwhelmed by the energy around them, unsure of how to protect themselves or how to navigate relationships without losing their sense of self. The emotional toll of these experiences can lead to burnout, anxiety, and a sense of hopelessness.

The Journey from Vulnerability to Empowerment

Despite the many challenges empaths face, it is important to remember that vulnerability does not equate to weakness. While empaths are often more susceptible to the emotional ups and downs of the world around them, their gift of empathy can also be their greatest strength. The journey from vulnerability to empowerment begins with recognizing and accepting this truth.

Empowerment for an empath involves learning how to manage and protect their emotional energy, to set clear boundaries, and to take control of their emotional well-being. It is about transforming vulnerability into strength and using their natural sensitivity as a tool for healing, both for themselves and for others.

The journey to empowerment starts with self-awareness. Embracing the empath's sensitivity as a unique gift—rather than a burden—lays the foundation for healing and transformation. In this book, we will explore ways to help empaths tap into their inner strength and develop the emotional resilience needed to thrive in a world that often feels emotionally toxic. Through the ten steps outlined in this guide, you will learn to:

1. **Recognize toxic relationships**: Understanding the signs of toxic and narcissistic behaviors will help you identify when you are being manipulated or drained emotionally.

2. **Protect your energy**: Learn how to create emotional boundaries that preserve your energy and prevent emotional burnout.

3. **Trust your intuition**: Developing trust in your own emotional insights can guide you in making healthier decisions and avoiding harmful situations.

4. **Empower yourself through self-care**: Embrace practices that nourish your mind, body, and soul, allowing you to recharge and protect your emotional health.

5. **Set healthy boundaries**: Establish clear, firm boundaries that preserve your well-being and help you create healthier, more balanced relationships.

6. **Shift your mindset**: Transition from feelings of powerlessness to a mindset of empowerment, where you take control of your emotional health.

7. **Cultivate emotional resilience**: Develop the tools necessary to handle emotional challenges with grace and strength, without compromising your core values.

8. **Create supportive relationships**: Surround yourself with people who uplift and support you, rather than drain your energy.

9. **Release toxic attachments**: Learn to recognize when it's time to let go of relationships that no longer serve your highest good.

10. **Embrace your gift of empathy**: Rather than seeing your sensitivity as a vulnerability, learn

to embrace it as a source of strength and personal power.

As empaths, we are naturally predisposed to care deeply for others. But in order to truly help those around us, we must first learn to care for ourselves. By embarking on this journey of self-discovery and empowerment, you will learn to break free from the toxic relationships that drain your energy and sense of self. You will discover how to stand firm in your own emotional truth, and to build relationships that are rooted in mutual respect, understanding, and love.

This book is not just a guide for surviving toxic relationships—it is a blueprint for thriving in a world that often feels emotionally exhausting and draining. It is a call to all empaths to embrace their gifts, protect their energy, and live with the knowledge that their vulnerability is, in fact, the key to their greatest strength. The journey may not always be easy, but by taking the first step toward empowerment, you are already on your way to a life of emotional freedom and inner peace.

Breaking Free

Welcome to your journey of breaking free.

Peter Sanglass

Chapter 1: Understanding Narcissism and Empathy

In our interconnected world, relationships are an essential aspect of our well-being. However, not all relationships are nourishing or healthy. For empaths, navigating relationships can be especially challenging, particularly when they find themselves drawn into toxic connections with narcissistic individuals. The dynamic between empaths and narcissists is one that is both complex and draining, yet understanding the characteristics of both narcissism and empathy can help empaths protect themselves and regain control of their emotional lives.

In this chapter, we will dive deep into two seemingly opposing yet interconnected concepts: narcissism and empathy. We will explore the traits of narcissistic individuals, different types of narcissistic personalities, and how these individuals interact with empaths. We will also examine the nature of empathy, the unique challenges empaths face, and why they are particularly vulnerable to narcissistic manipulation. Finally, we will explore the dynamics of narcissist-empath relationships, the patterns that emerge, and the emotional toll these relationships can take.

What is Narcissism?

Narcissism, in its simplest definition, refers to an excessive preoccupation with oneself, an inflated sense of one's own importance, and a lack of genuine concern for others. The term "narcissism" is derived from Greek mythology, where Narcissus, a young man, fell in love with his own reflection in a pool of water, ultimately becoming obsessed with his image. This self-obsession is at the core of narcissistic personality traits.

Psychologists and mental health professionals classify narcissism as a personality disorder, known as Narcissistic Personality Disorder (NPD). According to the Diagnostic and Statistical Manual of Mental Disorders (DSM-5), the diagnosis of NPD requires the presence of at least five of the following traits:

1. **Grandiosity** – An exaggerated sense of self-importance and an expectation of admiration from others.

2. **Preoccupation with fantasies of unlimited success, power, brilliance, or beauty.**

3. **Believing that they are special or unique and should only associate with other high-status individuals or institutions.**

4. **Requiring excessive admiration and attention.**

5. **A sense of entitlement**, expecting favorable treatment and compliance with their desires.

6. **Being interpersonally exploitative**, taking advantage of others for personal gain.

7. **Lacking empathy** – An inability to recognize or care about the feelings and needs of others.

8. **Being frequently envious of others or believing that others are envious of them.**

9. **Demonstrating arrogant or haughty behaviors or attitudes.**

While narcissism exists on a spectrum, with some individuals displaying mild narcissistic traits, Narcissistic Personality Disorder is the most extreme form. Narcissists are often highly manipulative and skilled at using their charm to gain control over others. However, they lack true emotional depth, and their relationships tend to be superficial and transactional.

Traits of Narcissistic Individuals

Understanding narcissism means recognizing the behaviors and traits that define narcissistic individuals. These individuals may appear outwardly confident, charming, and successful, but this veneer of self-assurance often masks their deeper insecurities and emotional deficiencies. Some key traits of narcissistic individuals include:

1. Exaggerated sense of self-importance

Narcissists often inflate their accomplishments, talents, or achievements, and they believe that they are superior to others. They crave constant admiration and may boast about their perceived greatness, often without any basis in reality.

2. Lack of empathy

A fundamental aspect of narcissism is the inability or unwillingness to empathize with others. Narcissists rarely consider how their actions affect those around them. They are primarily focused on their own needs, desires, and emotions, and they often dismiss or minimize the feelings of others.

3. Manipulation and exploitation

Narcissists are often adept at manipulating others to fulfill their own needs. They use tactics like guilt-tripping, gaslighting, and emotional coercion to control people and ensure their continued supply of admiration, attention, and validation.

4. Need for admiration

Narcissists thrive on attention and admiration. They often surround themselves with people who will praise them and make them feel important. This need for constant validation can lead them to seek out relationships where they can maintain the upper hand and control the narrative.

5. Fragile self-esteem

Although narcissists appear confident and self-assured on the outside, their sense of self-worth is often fragile. They are highly sensitive to criticism and may react with rage or defensiveness when their grandiose self-image is challenged.

6. Sense of entitlement

Narcissists believe that they deserve special treatment and are entitled to things that others may not have. This sense of entitlement often extends to their relationships, where they may expect others to cater to their needs without offering anything in return.

7. Arrogance and superiority

Narcissists often act as if they are above others, belittling those around them and looking down on those they consider "inferior." Their arrogance is a defense mechanism to protect themselves from their deep-seated insecurities.

Types of Narcissistic Personalities

While Narcissistic Personality Disorder manifests in many ways, there are different types of narcissists, each with their own distinct characteristics. Understanding these types can help empaths recognize the specific challenges they might face when interacting with narcissistic individuals.

1. Grandiose Narcissists

These narcissists are the most overt in their behavior. They are bold, confident, and often boast about their accomplishments. They demand admiration and attention and are typically aggressive in pursuing their goals. They may come across as charming, but their self-centeredness and need for validation drive their actions.

2. Vulnerable Narcissists

In contrast to the grandiose narcissist, vulnerable narcissists are more introverted and fragile. They may present themselves as shy or reserved, but they still have an inflated sense of self-worth. They often feel victimized or misunderstood and may seek validation by eliciting sympathy from others. Vulnerable narcissists tend to be more passive-aggressive in their manipulation tactics.

3. Covert Narcissists

Covert narcissists are often subtle in their manipulation. They may not openly demand admiration or attention but instead use passive methods such as guilt-tripping or playing the victim to elicit emotional responses from others. They often appear humble or self-deprecating but still have a deep need for validation and a sense of superiority.

4. Malignant Narcissists

Malignant narcissists are the most dangerous type. In addition to the typical narcissistic traits, they exhibit antisocial behaviors such as deceit, cruelty, and aggression. They are often manipulative, vindictive, and lack any remorse for their actions. They may engage in abusive behaviors and derive satisfaction from hurting others.

What is Empathy?

Empathy is the ability to understand, recognize, and share the emotions of others. It is the capacity to put oneself in another person's shoes and feel what they are feeling. Empathy is essential for healthy relationships because it enables individuals to connect emotionally, show compassion, and provide support.

Empathy is not the same as sympathy. While sympathy involves feeling pity or sorrow for someone else's suffering, empathy goes a step further. It involves experiencing another person's emotions as if they were your own, allowing you to truly understand their experience and respond with compassion.

The Gift and Burden of Being an Empath

For empaths, the ability to feel the emotions of others is both a gift and a burden. On one hand, empaths are incredibly compassionate, intuitive, and capable of forming deep, meaningful connections with others. They have an innate understanding of the emotional states of those around them, which allows them to offer support, comfort, and healing. Empaths are often drawn to careers in caregiving, counseling, and healing because they derive fulfillment from helping others.

On the other hand, being an empath can be emotionally draining. Because empaths absorb the emotions of others, they are vulnerable to emotional burnout. They may feel overwhelmed by the intensity of others' feelings, particularly in toxic or manipulative relationships. Constantly giving of themselves without receiving the same level of care and consideration can lead to exhaustion, anxiety, and a diminished sense of self.

The empathy that allows empaths to connect with others also makes them susceptible to emotional exploitation. Narcissists, in particular, are drawn to empaths because they are easy targets for manipulation. The empath's desire to help, heal, and nurture can be used against them, leaving them emotionally depleted and confused.

How Empaths Attract Narcissists

Empaths and narcissists often find themselves in relationships with each other because they fulfill opposite needs. The empath's nurturing nature and deep capacity for understanding provide the narcissist with the emotional validation and admiration they crave. Conversely, the narcissist's self-centeredness and need for control appeal to the empath's desire to help and fix others. This dynamic creates an imbalance, with the empath often giving more than they receive.

Empaths tend to attract narcissists because they are compassionate and empathetic, which makes them easy to manipulate. Narcissists quickly recognize an empath's vulnerability and emotional openness, seeing these qualities as an opportunity to exploit the empath's desire to please and care for others. The empath may find themselves drawn to the narcissist's charm, only to later realize that they are being emotionally drained and manipulated.

The Dynamics of Narcissist-Empath Relationships

The relationship between a narcissist and an empath is a toxic, one-sided dynamic that can cause significant emotional damage to the empath. The narcissist's need for admiration and control is met through the empath's constant giving and caretaking. However, this relationship is unsustainable, as the empath eventually becomes emotionally depleted and overwhelmed.

Why Opposites Attract and Clash

The narcissist and empath are polar opposites in many ways, but these differences often create an intense attraction. The narcissist is drawn to the empath's sensitivity and willingness to provide emotional validation, while the empath is attracted to the narcissist's confidence and charm. However, over time, these differences begin to clash.

The narcissist's emotional manipulation and lack of empathy gradually wear down the empath's sense of self-worth. The empath's constant giving without receiving the same level of care creates an emotional imbalance. As the narcissist demands more and more attention, the empath becomes emotionally drained, leading to feelings of resentment and confusion.

The Cycle of Manipulation and Emotional Drain

The relationship between a narcissist and an empath often follows a predictable cycle of manipulation and emotional drain. Initially, the narcissist may shower the empath with love-bombing—intense affection, praise, and attention meant to win their trust and devotion. Once the empath is fully invested in the relationship, the narcissist begins to devalue them, using tactics like gaslighting, belittling, and emotional withdrawal to maintain control.

The empath, driven by their desire to help and please, continues to give, often sacrificing their own emotional needs in the process. Over time, this pattern of manipulation leads to emotional exhaustion and a diminished sense of self-worth for the empath. The narcissist, meanwhile, continues to extract energy and admiration without ever offering true emotional support in return.

In the following chapters, we will explore how empaths can break free from this cycle of emotional drain by recognizing toxic behaviors, setting healthy boundaries, and reclaiming their emotional power.

Conclusion

In this chapter, we have explored the complex dynamics of narcissism and empathy, delving into how these two forces interact and shape relationships. Narcissism, with its self-centered traits and lack of empathy, presents a profound challenge for those who possess the opposite qualities—empaths. Empaths, who are inherently attuned to the emotions and needs of others, often find themselves drawn to narcissistic individuals, despite the toxicity that may lurk beneath the surface.

Understanding the traits and behaviors of narcissists is crucial for empaths to recognize the red flags and avoid the traps of manipulation, gaslighting, and emotional depletion. Narcissists thrive on control and admiration, leaving their partners feeling drained, confused, and undervalued. On the other hand, empaths possess an extraordinary ability to connect deeply with others, but this sensitivity can also leave them vulnerable to emotional exploitation.

However, as we've learned, the interplay between narcissism and empathy is not merely one of victim and perpetrator—it is a dynamic that empaths can learn to navigate with awareness, strength, and resilience. By recognizing the patterns and behaviors of narcissists, empaths can begin to reclaim their emotional sovereignty, protect their energy, and take the first steps toward healthier, more balanced relationships.

This chapter serves as the foundation for the journey ahead, equipping empaths with the knowledge to understand their vulnerability and the narcissistic individuals they may encounter. The deeper understanding of these dynamics will help guide you through the complexities of relationships, offering tools to break free from toxic patterns and ultimately thrive in a world that can often be overwhelming.

As we move forward, the key takeaway is clear: understanding both narcissism and empathy is the first step in breaking free from harmful cycles, and it is the foundation upon which true healing and empowerment can begin. With this knowledge, empaths can step into their power and start the process of transforming vulnerability into strength.

Chapter 1 Key Takeaways

Narcissism is a personality trait characterized by a lack of empathy, a need for admiration, and an inflated sense of self-importance.

Traits of Narcissistic Individuals: They often exhibit manipulative behavior, a sense of entitlement, and disregard for others' emotions or boundaries.

Types of Narcissistic Personalities: There are grandiose narcissists (overly arrogant and self-absorbed) and vulnerable narcissists (more sensitive but still self-centered and manipulative).

Empathy involves recognizing and sharing the feelings of others, making empaths deeply sensitive to others' emotions.

The Gift and Burden of Being an Empath: While empaths have the ability to deeply connect with others, this can make them vulnerable to being manipulated by narcissists.

Empaths Attracting Narcissists: Narcissists are drawn to empaths due to their emotional openness and willingness to care for others.

The Narcissist-Empath Dynamic: The relationship often involves manipulation, emotional drain, and unhealthy dependency. Empaths may feel overwhelmed, while narcissists feed off their emotional energy.

Real-Life Applications

Identifying Narcissism and Empathy

- **Prompt:** Write down five traits of narcissists and five traits of empaths. Reflect on how these traits have shown up in your relationships.

- **Example:**

    o Narcissist traits: Manipulative, lacks empathy, grandiose, seeks constant validation, dismissive of others' feelings.

o Empath traits: Deeply caring, highly intuitive, emotionally attuned, self-sacrificing, compassionate.

o **Reflection:** "I've noticed how my compassion often draws me to people who need constant validation, making me feel drained."

Chapter 2: Recognizing the Signs of Toxic Relationships

In the journey of navigating relationships, it can be challenging to distinguish between healthy dynamics and toxic ones, especially when it involves individuals with narcissistic tendencies or emotionally manipulative behaviors. This chapter will delve into recognizing the key signs of toxic relationships, from emotional manipulation and gaslighting to understanding emotional abuse, subtle and overt abuse tactics, and the crucial role of intuition in safeguarding one's emotional well-being. By learning to identify these behaviors early, you will be empowered to protect your emotional health and break free from unhealthy patterns.

Red Flags in Relationships

Relationships, whether romantic, familial, or professional, should be built on mutual respect, trust, and support. However, not all relationships operate within these healthy parameters. Toxic relationships are often marked by patterns of emotional manipulation, control, and exploitation. Understanding the red flags that indicate a relationship is becoming or has already become toxic is essential for empaths, who are often more vulnerable to these dynamics due to their heightened sensitivity and desire to nurture others.

Emotional Manipulation and Gaslighting

One of the most common and insidious tactics employed in toxic relationships is **emotional manipulation**. This behavior involves using emotions to control or influence another person. It often includes guilt-tripping, shaming, or making the other person feel responsible for the manipulator's emotions or actions. Narcissists, in particular, are skilled at this form of manipulation, as they seek to control the emotional energy of those around them.

Gaslighting, a term that originates from a 1938 play and its subsequent film adaptations, is a form of emotional manipulation designed to make the victim doubt their own perception of reality. A narcissist might use gaslighting to make the empath feel like they are overreacting, imagining things, or misunderstanding the situation. Over time, this tactic can severely undermine an empath's sense of self and make them question their own intuition and feelings. Examples of gaslighting in relationships include:

- **Denial of actions or words**: The narcissist may deny saying something hurtful or even blame the empath for making up the conversation, causing confusion.

- **Rewriting history**: Narcissists may twist past events to make the empath appear at fault, creating a warped version of reality that further isolates the empath.

- **Dismissal of feelings**: The narcissist may minimize or invalidate the empath's feelings, telling them that they are being "too sensitive" or "dramatic."

Gaslighting can be a particularly dangerous form of emotional manipulation because it chips away at an empath's ability to trust themselves. As the empath becomes more confused, they begin to rely on the narcissist's version of reality, which deepens their emotional dependence on the narcissist.

Lack of Reciprocity and Excessive Demands

In a healthy relationship, both individuals contribute to the emotional and physical needs of the other. There is a balance of give and take, where both parties feel valued, heard, and supported. However, in toxic relationships, one person typically becomes the emotional caretaker, and the other becomes a perpetual taker, draining energy without offering anything in return.

Narcissistic individuals, for example, often demand excessive attention and admiration, leaving little room for the empath's own needs. The empath may feel overwhelmed by the narcissist's constant emotional demands, yet when they try to express their own needs, they are met with indifference, criticism, or outright hostility.

Some signs of a lack of reciprocity include:

- **One-sided communication**: Conversations always revolve around the narcissist, with little interest in the empath's life or feelings.

- **Emotional withdrawal**: When the empath is upset or in need of support, the narcissist may ignore them, dismiss their feelings, or turn the situation around to focus on their own issues.

- **Guilt-tripping**: The narcissist may make the empath feel guilty for having needs or for taking time for themselves. The empath may be made to feel selfish for requesting attention or care.

- **Unmet emotional needs**: The empath may constantly sacrifice their own well-being for the narcissist, but the narcissist never reciprocates this care. In fact, they may actively avoid providing emotional support.

Over time, the empath begins to feel emotionally drained, unimportant, and unseen. They may doubt their own worth, feeling as if they are not deserving of kindness or emotional care. This imbalance in a relationship can create a toxic dynamic where the empath continually gives and gives, yet the narcissist continues to take without ever offering anything in return.

How to Identify Emotional Abuse

Emotional abuse can be one of the most difficult forms of abuse to recognize, as it often happens behind closed doors and may not leave visible scars. However, the effects of emotional abuse can be deeply damaging to an empath's mental and emotional well-being. Understanding the signs of emotional abuse is crucial in identifying and addressing toxic relationships.

Subtle vs. Overt Abuse Tactics

Emotional abuse can manifest in both **subtle** and **overt** ways. Subtle abuse tactics often begin slowly and can be hard to detect, as they are masked by seemingly innocent behaviors or words. Overt abuse, on the other hand, is more direct and aggressive.

Subtle Abuse Tactics

- **Passive-aggressive behavior**: Instead of openly addressing issues, the narcissist may use passive-aggressive behavior, such as giving the silent treatment, making snide comments, or sabotaging the empath's efforts.

- **Backhanded compliments**: Narcissists often disguise insults as compliments, creating confusion for the empath. For example, "You look great for your age" is meant to flatter, but it also subtly undermines the empath's confidence.

- **Undermining self-esteem**: The narcissist may subtly undermine the empath's sense of self-worth by constantly pointing out their flaws or making them feel inadequate. This might involve comments like, "You're lucky I put up with you," or "I'm the only one who understands you."

- **Controlling behaviors**: The narcissist may subtly control aspects of the empath's life, such as dictating who they can see, where they can go, or what they can do, all under the guise of "concern" or "love."

Overt Abuse Tactics

- **Verbal insults and criticism**: The narcissist may openly belittle, insult, or criticize the empath, often in front of others, to make them feel inferior or ashamed.

- **Blaming and accusing**: The narcissist will often accuse the empath of things they haven't done or blame them for problems in the relationship, even when it is the narcissist's behavior that is at fault.

- **Emotional outbursts**: Narcissists may throw tantrums, scream, or become aggressive when they feel their ego is threatened. This behavior is meant to intimidate the empath and reinforce their sense of control.

- **Threats and intimidation**: In extreme cases, the narcissist may threaten the empath with physical harm, blackmail, or other forms of intimidation to keep them under control.

Whether subtle or overt, emotional abuse has one goal: to control and dominate the empath. Over time, the empath begins to lose their sense of self, internalizing the negative messages from the narcissist and feeling trapped in a cycle of manipulation.

Understanding Your Triggers and Vulnerabilities

Every individual has emotional triggers—specific things that, when said or done, cause a strong emotional reaction. For empaths, these triggers can be especially intense because they feel the emotions of others deeply. Narcissists often prey on these triggers, using them to manipulate and control their victims.

Some common emotional triggers for empaths include:

- **Feeling ignored or unimportant**: Narcissists often ignore or dismiss the empath's feelings, triggering a sense of abandonment or worthlessness in the empath.

- **Feeling unappreciated**: When the empath goes unrecognized or unappreciated for their efforts, it can trigger feelings of inadequacy or low self-worth.

- **Feeling responsible for others' emotions**: Empaths often feel responsible for the emotional well-being of those around them. Narcissists exploit this vulnerability, making the empath feel guilty or obligated to meet their demands, even at the expense of their own well-being.

- **Fear of rejection**: Narcissists may use the threat of rejection to manipulate the empath, knowing that empaths have a deep-seated fear of being abandoned or unloved.

Recognizing your own emotional triggers and understanding how they can be used against you is an important step in reclaiming your emotional power. By becoming more self-aware and strengthening your emotional boundaries, you can begin to protect yourself from manipulation and emotional abuse.

The Role of Intuition

Empaths are often highly intuitive, meaning they have a strong, almost instinctual ability to sense the emotions of others. This intuitive capacity is a powerful tool when navigating relationships, as it can provide critical insight into a person's true intentions. However, narcissists are masters of deception and often put on a façade of charm and charisma, making it difficult for empaths to discern authenticity from manipulation.

Trusting Your Gut Feelings

One of the most important tools in recognizing toxic relationships is **trusting your gut feelings**. Empaths often have an innate sense of when something is "off" in a relationship, even when everything seems fine on the surface. This feeling of discomfort is your intuition speaking, trying to warn you that something is not right.

Signs that your gut feelings might be telling you something is wrong include:

- **Feeling drained** after interactions with a particular person.

- **A sense of unease** or anxiety that lingers after spending time with them.

- **Doubts or confusion** about the other person's intentions or words.

- **Physical discomfort** such as tension, tightness in your chest, or stomach problems when you are around this person.

It's essential to trust these feelings and give them the space to guide your actions. If something doesn't feel right, it is worth investigating further, whether by observing the person's behavior more closely, seeking advice from trusted friends, or setting healthy boundaries with the individual.

How to Discern Authenticity in Others

While intuition is a powerful tool, it's also important to learn how to discern authenticity in others. Narcissists are often skilled at projecting an image of themselves that aligns with what others want to see. However, beneath the surface, their true intentions may be quite different.

To discern authenticity in others, ask yourself the following questions:

- **Do their actions match their words?** Pay attention to inconsistencies between what the person says and what they do. Narcissists may promise one thing but consistently fail to follow through.

- **Do they respect your boundaries?** Authentic people respect the emotional boundaries of others, whereas narcissists often push against them.

- **Do they take responsibility for their actions?** Narcissists rarely take responsibility for their actions, often blaming others for their mistakes or shortcomings.

- **Are they empathetic?** Authentic individuals show empathy and understanding for others' feelings, while narcissists tend to dismiss or belittle others' emotions.

By carefully observing others' behaviors and being attuned to your own feelings, you can more easily recognize when someone is not being authentic and when they may be trying to manipulate you.

Conclusion

Recognizing the signs of toxic relationships is an essential step in protecting your emotional health and well-being. Emotional manipulation, gaslighting, lack of reciprocity, and emotional abuse are all tactics that narcissistic individuals use to control and exploit others. Empaths, with their heightened sensitivity and desire to help, are often prime targets for these behaviors. However, by becoming aware of these red flags, learning to trust your intuition, and understanding your own emotional triggers, you can begin to set boundaries and reclaim your power. In the following chapters, we will explore how to establish and maintain these boundaries, break free from toxic patterns, and empower yourself to thrive in healthier relationships.

Chapter 2 Takeaways

Red Flags in relationships often include emotional manipulation, gaslighting, and a lack of reciprocity.

Emotional Manipulation and Gaslighting: Narcissists use tactics to distort reality, causing the empath to doubt their perceptions and question their sanity.

Lack of Reciprocity: Narcissists demand excessive attention and energy while offering little in return.

Identifying Emotional Abuse: Abuse can be subtle, such as emotional neglect or verbal manipulation, and may be difficult to recognize.

Subtle vs. Overt Abuse: Recognizing both the overt and more insidious forms of abuse is essential for self-protection.

Understanding Your Triggers and Vulnerabilities: Awareness of emotional triggers helps empaths protect themselves from manipulation and emotional exhaustion.

Role of Intuition: Empaths often have a strong sense of intuition, which can be key to recognizing toxic situations and individuals.

Real-Life Applications

Spotting Red Flags

- **Prompt:** Create a list of 10 potential red flags in relationships. Reflect on which ones you've encountered and how they made you feel.

- **Example:**

    o Red flags: Gaslighting, controlling behavior, lack of accountability, excessive criticism, isolating me from others.

o **Reflection:** "My last relationship showed several red flags, like gaslighting and constant criticism, which made me question my self-worth."

Chapter 3: Building Healthy Boundaries

In the realm of personal development and emotional health, **boundaries** are essential for maintaining a healthy, balanced life. For empaths, building and maintaining strong boundaries can be especially challenging due to their heightened sensitivity and desire to help others. In this chapter, we will explore the importance of boundaries, why empaths struggle with saying "no," the consequences of having porous boundaries, and how to set and enforce boundaries effectively. You'll learn practical tips for asserting yourself, how to deal with guilt and resistance, and the techniques for communicating your boundaries in a calm yet firm way. We'll also address how to recognize and handle pushback from those who may try to test or break your boundaries.

The Importance of Boundaries

Boundaries are emotional, mental, and physical limits we establish to protect ourselves from being overwhelmed or mistreated by others. They are essential for maintaining our well-being and self-respect, and they define where we end and where others begin. Healthy boundaries help us prioritize our needs, manage our energy, and cultivate relationships that are balanced, supportive, and respectful. For empaths, who often feel the emotions and energies of others deeply, boundaries are particularly important in preventing burnout, emotional exhaustion, and exploitation.

Protecting Your Emotional Well-being

Boundaries are about **self-care** and protecting your emotional health. For empaths, this protection is critical because they tend to absorb the emotions of others, often leaving them feeling emotionally depleted. Without boundaries, an empath may unintentionally allow others to take more than their fair share of emotional energy. For example, empathic individuals can sometimes take on the weight of others' burdens and struggles, even when they're not in a position to help. Over time, this will result in feelings of emotional exhaustion, overwhelm, and burnout.

Without clear boundaries, an empath risks neglecting their own emotional needs in favor of helping others. The cost of this neglect is significant. Recharging, taking breaks, and focusing on your own emotional health are essential for long-term well-being.

Preserving Your Energy

One of the most fundamental purposes of boundaries is to **preserve your energy**. In the case of empaths, this is paramount. Constantly giving of yourself to others without taking time to replenish your own resources can quickly lead to emotional and physical depletion. When empaths do not set boundaries, they allow others to take from their reserves without replenishing them. This can result in a chronic state of exhaustion, where the empath feels drained, unmotivated, or mentally foggy.

By setting boundaries, you ensure that you have enough energy to give to the things that matter most, whether that's your loved ones, your career, or your personal growth. When you protect your energy, you create the space for meaningful interactions with others, while ensuring you have enough resources to care for yourself.

Cultivating Respectful Relationships

Healthy boundaries create a foundation for **mutual respect** in relationships. Relationships, whether they are personal or professional, require balance. Without boundaries, one party can dominate or drain the other, creating an unhealthy dynamic. For empaths, this is particularly challenging, as they are naturally inclined to give more of themselves than they receive.

When boundaries are clearly communicated and respected, both individuals in a relationship can feel valued. Healthy boundaries ensure that your emotional needs are respected while also honoring the needs of the other person. Setting boundaries doesn't mean you are pushing people away; it means that you are cultivating relationships that are balanced, where both people contribute to the well-being of the other.

Why Empaths Struggle with Saying "No"

For many empaths, saying "no" can feel nearly impossible. This is often because empaths have a deep desire to help others, offer support, and avoid causing conflict. Their high emotional sensitivity leads them to internalize the feelings of others, and they may feel compelled to say "yes" to requests, even when it's not in their best interest. There are several reasons why empaths struggle with saying "no":

Fear of Rejection or Abandonment

Empaths often fear that saying "no" will lead to **rejection** or **abandonment**. Because they feel others' emotions so deeply, they may interpret a refusal as a personal attack or a sign that they are unworthy of love and connection. This fear can make it difficult to set boundaries, as the empath may prioritize the other person's emotional needs over their own. They worry that if they don't help or comply, the person will stop loving or valuing them.

However, saying "no" is not a rejection of the person —it is a healthy assertion of your own needs. This fear of rejection can be tied to deeper emotional issues, such as childhood experiences of neglect or abandonment, where an empath learned that their worth was tied to their ability to be accommodating and helpful. Learning to recognize and separate these feelings from the reality of a situation is key to overcoming this fear.

Overwhelming Empathy

Empaths naturally put others' feelings before their own. When someone asks for help or support, they often feel an intense emotional pull to assist. This overwhelming empathy can make it hard for empaths to set limits, as they don't want to let anyone down or cause them distress. For instance, an empath may take on the emotional burdens of a friend or loved one, even when it becomes overwhelming, simply because they don't want to see that person suffer.

However, this emotional intensity can be draining. The act of constantly taking on the emotional weight of others can lead to emotional exhaustion, resentment, and burnout. It is crucial for empaths to learn to create emotional distance, recognizing that while they can offer support, they are not responsible for another person's feelings or well-being.

Guilt and People-Pleasing

Many empaths have been conditioned to be **people-pleasers**, often seeking validation through service or helping others. They may feel a deep sense of **guilt** when they cannot accommodate others' needs, believing that saying "no" makes them selfish or unkind. This guilt can be paralyzing, leading them to continue giving, even when it is detrimental to their well-being. The need to please others often arises from a fear of conflict or rejection, leading the empath to abandon their own needs in favor of others.

Empaths may have learned, early in life, that their value comes from being helpful or accommodating. This is especially true in environments where their needs were neglected or where emotional manipulation was a pattern. Overcoming people-pleasing behaviors requires deep self-reflection and a commitment to learning to prioritize one's own needs.

Difficulty Recognizing Their Own Needs

Empaths often focus so much on others that they lose sight of their own needs. Without clear boundaries, it becomes difficult for an empath to recognize when they are overwhelmed, exhausted, or emotionally drained. They may simply accept more responsibilities or demands from others without considering their own limits, which causes them to stretch themselves thin.

Empaths may also struggle with identifying their own emotions, as they are so accustomed to picking up on the emotions of others. This can lead to confusion about what they truly need or desire. Being able to tune into one's own emotional and physical state is essential for understanding when it's time to set a boundary.

The Consequences of Porous Boundaries

When empaths fail to establish strong boundaries, they risk emotional burnout, resentment, and a loss of self-identity. The consequences of porous boundaries are profound and can affect all areas of life.

Emotional Exhaustion

One of the most immediate consequences of weak boundaries is **emotional exhaustion**. Empaths may find themselves constantly drained by the emotional demands of others, leaving little energy for self-care or relaxation. When you say "yes" to everyone else, you leave yourself with nothing—no time, no energy, and no space for your own emotions. Over time, this can lead to burnout, anxiety, and even depression.

The signs of emotional exhaustion in empaths can manifest as feelings of irritability, mood swings, and a general sense of being overwhelmed. There may also be physical symptoms such as fatigue, headaches, or insomnia. Emotional exhaustion can affect all areas of life, including relationships, work, and health.

Resentment and Anger

When you continuously put others' needs before your own, **resentment** begins to build. You may feel unappreciated, taken advantage of, or even trapped in relationships that require constant emotional labor. As this resentment builds, it can turn into **anger**, which may manifest in passive-aggressive behavior, outbursts, or a sense of bitterness toward others.

While empaths tend to avoid confrontation, the inability to set boundaries may result in an outburst or withdrawal. Resentment can also cause emotional distance in relationships, as the empath may start to feel like they are giving too much and receiving too little. Healthy boundaries help to prevent these negative feelings from escalating.

Loss of Self-Identity

One of the most insidious effects of porous boundaries is the gradual **loss of self-identity**. Empaths who continuously prioritize others may lose touch with their own needs, desires, and values. Over time, they can become so enmeshed with the needs of others that they forget who they are and what they want out of life. This identity loss can lead to feelings of emptiness, confusion, and a lack of direction.

Empaths who are constantly focusing on others may find it difficult to articulate their own desires, goals, or values. This lack of self-awareness can create a profound sense of disconnection, leading to feelings of depression or loneliness.

Enabling Toxic Behavior

Without clear boundaries, empaths may inadvertently **enable toxic or manipulative behavior** from others. Narcissists, for example, can take advantage of an empath's inability to say "no" and continuously exploit their energy and resources. Over time, the empath becomes trapped in a cycle of emotional depletion, enabling the narcissist to maintain control over the relationship.

Empaths are particularly vulnerable to manipulation in relationships with narcissists, as narcissists often prey on empaths' tendency to over-give and under-receive. Recognizing and establishing boundaries with toxic individuals is crucial for preventing further harm.

How to Set and Enforce Boundaries

Setting boundaries is an essential skill for empaths, but it's not always easy. It requires self-awareness, assertiveness, and a willingness to prioritize your own well-being. However, with practice and consistency, it is possible to establish boundaries that protect your emotional health without sacrificing the relationships that matter most.

Practical Tips for Asserting Yourself

1. **Know Your Limits**: Before you can set boundaries, it's important to understand your own limits. Pay attention to how you feel in different situations—when you're with certain people, doing specific tasks, or engaging in particular activities. Do you feel energized or drained? Are you overwhelmed or at peace? Recognizing your own emotional and physical limits will help you identify when it's time to say "no" or set a boundary.

2. **Be Clear and Specific**: When setting a boundary, be as clear and specific as possible. Avoid vague statements like "I can't right now" or "Maybe later." Instead, communicate your needs directly. For example, "I need some quiet time to recharge" or "I can't take on any more projects right now."

3. **Use "I" Statements**: Assertiveness comes from speaking in a way that reflects your own needs and feelings, rather than placing blame or making the other person responsible. For instance, "I feel overwhelmed when I take on too many tasks" or "I need to take care of myself before I can help you."

4. **Practice Saying "No"**: Saying "no" is a muscle that needs to be exercised. Start with small, low-stakes situations where you can practice saying no without feeling guilty. The more you practice, the easier it will become.

5. **Give Yourself Permission**: It's crucial to remember that you have the right to say "no." You don't need permission from anyone else

to prioritize your own well-being. Give yourself permission to establish boundaries that serve your health and happiness.

Dealing with Guilt and Resistance

Setting boundaries can bring up feelings of guilt, especially for empaths who are deeply attuned to the emotions of others. You may worry that you're being selfish or letting people down. However, it's important to reframe guilt as a natural response to change. Over time, the more you set boundaries, the less guilt you will feel.

Here are some strategies for dealing with guilt and resistance:

- **Challenge the guilt**: Remind yourself that setting boundaries is not selfish; it's necessary for your emotional health. By setting boundaries, you are teaching others how to treat you with respect, and you are preserving your ability to be there for others in a healthy way.

- **Acknowledge the discomfort**: Recognize that setting boundaries may be uncomfortable at first. The guilt, discomfort, or resistance you feel is normal, but it does not mean you're doing something wrong. It's simply part of the process.

- **Focus on the benefits**: Think about the long-term benefits of having healthy boundaries. By protecting your energy, you will be able to show up more fully in relationships and take better care of yourself.

- **Seek support**: It can be helpful to talk to a trusted friend or therapist about your struggles with setting boundaries. They can offer encouragement and perspective as you work through the discomfort.

Communicating Boundaries Effectively

Effective communication is key to maintaining healthy boundaries. Setting a boundary is only the first step—the next challenge is communicating that boundary in a way that others can understand and respect. Here are some techniques for having calm yet firm conversations about your boundaries:

1. **Be Direct but Gentle**: You can be firm in setting your boundaries without being harsh or aggressive. Use a calm tone and direct language to express your needs. For example, "I cannot take on any more responsibilities right now" or "I need some time alone to recharge."

2. **Stay Calm and Collected**: When you communicate your boundaries, try to remain calm and composed. If the other person gets upset or defensive, stay centered and don't get drawn into an emotional confrontation. You can acknowledge their feelings while still maintaining your boundary.

3. **Be Consistent**: Consistency is crucial when setting boundaries. If you allow someone to cross your boundaries once, they may assume it's okay to do so again. Stick to your limits and communicate them regularly.

4. **Be Prepared for Pushback**: Some people may resist or challenge your boundaries, especially if they are used to you being more

accommodating. Be prepared for this resistance, and remember that it's normal. Stick to your decision, and remain firm but respectful.

Recognizing and Addressing Pushback

Pushback is a natural part of setting boundaries, particularly with people who are used to having their way. Some common forms of pushback include:

- **Guilt-tripping**: The person may try to make you feel guilty for setting a boundary, often by saying things like, "I thought you cared about me," or "I really need your help."

- **Manipulation**: Some individuals may try to manipulate you by playing on your emotions or using flattery to get you to change your mind.

- **Anger or frustration**: If someone is used to you being accommodating, they may react with anger or frustration when you assert your boundaries.

When you encounter pushback, it's important to stay calm, avoid engaging in arguments, and remind the other person of your need for self-care. You don't owe anyone an explanation, but you can calmly reaffirm your boundaries. If necessary, walk away from the conversation or disengage from the person if they are being disrespectful.

Conclusion

Building healthy boundaries is a crucial skill for empaths, enabling them to protect their emotional health and cultivate balanced, respectful relationships. While it may be challenging at first, with practice and consistency, empaths can learn to set and enforce boundaries without guilt. By communicating your boundaries effectively, recognizing your triggers, and addressing pushback, you'll be able to reclaim your energy, prioritize your well-being, and create the space needed to thrive in all areas of life. Remember, boundaries are not walls; they are the foundation for healthy, thriving relationships, and ultimately, they serve to honor who you are and what you need.

Chapter 3 Takeaways

Importance of Boundaries: Boundaries are essential for protecting an empath's emotional health and ensuring their needs are met without overextending themselves.

Why Empaths Struggle with Saying "No": Empaths often feel guilty about setting boundaries, fearing rejection or conflict.

Consequences of Porous Boundaries: Without boundaries, empaths become emotionally depleted and may lose themselves in others' needs.

How to Set and Enforce Boundaries: It's important to practice asserting oneself calmly and without guilt, recognizing that setting boundaries is an act of self-respect.

Dealing with Guilt and Resistance: Overcoming feelings of guilt is a crucial part of boundary-setting, as is learning to navigate resistance from others.

Communicating Boundaries Effectively: Being firm but kind in expressing needs ensures that boundaries are respected, even when met with pushback.

Real-Life Applications

Practicing Boundaries

- **Prompt:** Role-play boundary-setting by writing a script for a hypothetical scenario, like saying "no" to an unreasonable request.

- **Example:**

    o Scenario: "A friend repeatedly asks me to help with tasks during my busy workdays."

    o Script: "I value our friendship, but I can't help during work hours. Let's plan another time that works for both of us."

Chapter 4: Healing from Emotional Wounds

Healing from emotional wounds is not just about moving on from the past; it's about transforming the pain into strength, reclaiming your sense of self, and learning to embrace life in a way that is authentic and full of possibility. For empaths, who tend to internalize the emotions and pain of others, the process of healing can sometimes feel complex and overwhelming. However, it is through the very act of healing that you will begin to reclaim your power, your sense of worth, and your capacity for joy and peace.

This chapter will delve further into the intricacies of healing from emotional wounds, focusing on several core themes: acknowledging your pain, moving past self-blame and shame, practicing self-compassion, seeking professional help, and learning effective techniques for rebuilding emotional health. Throughout this chapter, you will gain a deeper understanding of how to heal from emotional wounds in a way that is sustainable, loving, and transformative.

Acknowledging Your Pain: A Critical First Step

One of the most difficult, yet crucial, aspects of healing from emotional wounds is the ability to **acknowledge your pain**. Many empaths, particularly those who have suffered from toxic relationships, may have spent a significant portion of their lives ignoring or minimizing their emotional suffering. They may have been taught, either by direct experience or societal expectations, to put others first, often at the cost of their own emotional health.

The Importance of Recognizing and Naming Your Pain

When an empath finally acknowledges their pain, it can feel like a revelation. Naming the emotions you're feeling is an important first step in the healing process. It allows you to fully experience your emotions and begin the process of releasing them. **Naming your pain**—whether it's grief, anger, loneliness, or fear—gives you permission to feel what you need to feel. It allows you to honor your emotional experience rather than suppressing it.

For example, if you have suffered emotional abuse in a past relationship, recognizing the pain that abuse caused is not only necessary for healing, but it's also a way to affirm your own truth. It's vital to realize that acknowledging your pain is not a sign of weakness, but an act of courage. It demonstrates an understanding that healing cannot begin without fully confronting what has been lost, damaged, or ignored.

The Emotional Burden of Repressing Pain

When pain is left unaddressed, it can manifest in physical, mental, and emotional symptoms. **Unresolved trauma** may cause an empath to experience anxiety, depression, physical illness, and other stress-related disorders. These symptoms arise because the body and mind are carrying unresolved emotional weight that has never been fully processed.

Repressing pain can also contribute to **emotional numbness**, where an empath may feel disconnected from their own feelings or from the world around them. This state of emotional detachment can be a form of self-protection but can also prevent you from living a full and authentic life. Healing begins with honoring the pain, rather than pushing it aside, and understanding that emotions are signals to be heard, not avoided.

Moving Past Self-Blame and Shame

For empaths, particularly those who have been in toxic relationships or who have experienced trauma, **self-blame** and **shame** are often deeply ingrained. These feelings can become a significant obstacle in the healing process, as they distort one's perception of themselves and their worth.

Recognizing the Root of Self-Blame

Empaths often believe they are responsible for the pain they've experienced, particularly in toxic relationships. The tendency to absorb others' emotions means that empaths sometimes take on the emotional weight of the people around them. If a relationship becomes abusive or unhealthy, an empath may feel that they somehow caused it or failed to prevent it. The trauma of being in a toxic relationship can trigger feelings of inadequacy, leading the empath to wonder, "What did I do wrong?" or "If only I had done things differently."

Self-blame is often tied to the belief that you, as an empath, should have been able to fix the other person, make the relationship work, or prevent the emotional hurt from happening in the first place. The reality, however, is that **you are not responsible for the actions of others**, and it's important to release any feelings of guilt related to their behavior.

Releasing Shame

Shame is another insidious emotion that many empaths struggle with. It's not just about feeling guilty for something you've done; it's the belief that there is something inherently wrong with who you are. Shame can be devastating, especially for an empath, as it often stems from the belief that you are unworthy of love, respect, or happiness.

Releasing shame is a multifaceted process that takes time, self-compassion, and support. It involves challenging negative self-talk and changing the belief that you are "flawed" or "unlovable." It requires recognizing that your experiences—no matter how painful—do not define your worth. You can acknowledge the hurt, but that doesn't make you less valuable as a person.

Therapeutic practices such as **cognitive behavioral therapy (CBT)** and **trauma-focused therapy** can be incredibly helpful for empaths in shifting their perspective on shame. By reframing negative beliefs and learning healthier ways of thinking, you can begin to heal from shame and reclaim your sense of self-worth.

Practicing Self-Compassion

Self-compassion is the cornerstone of healing from emotional wounds. For many empaths, **self-compassion** can feel like an unfamiliar concept. They are often so focused on caring for others that they neglect their own emotional needs. However, without **self-compassion**, healing is not possible. If you do not treat yourself with the same care and kindness that you offer to others, the process of healing will be stalled.

Techniques to Cultivate Self-Compassion

1. **Mindful Self-Awareness**: The practice of mindfulness helps empaths become aware of their thoughts and emotions without judgment. Being mindful means observing your emotional states without labeling them as "good" or "bad." Mindfulness teaches you to accept your feelings as they are, without pushing them away or getting overwhelmed by them. This non-judgmental approach allows you to feel compassion for yourself, as you begin to recognize that all emotions—whether painful or joyful—are valid.

2. **Self-Compassionate Meditation**: This form of meditation involves focusing on feelings of warmth and kindness toward oneself. By visualizing a compassionate presence within or repeating phrases like "May I be happy," "May I be healthy," or "May I live with ease," empaths can foster feelings of self-compassion and acceptance. These meditations help break through the walls of self-criticism and

encourage a gentler, more loving approach toward oneself.

3. **Gentle Self-Talk**: One of the most powerful ways to practice self-compassion is by changing the way you speak to yourself. When you feel hurt or vulnerable, speak to yourself as you would to a close friend. Instead of saying, "I'm so stupid for letting that happen," try "I did the best I could with the information I had at the time." Replace harsh criticism with understanding and love.

4. **Physical Self-Care**: Self-compassion is not only an internal practice but also an external one. Taking care of your body is an essential component of emotional healing. Regular exercise, healthy eating, adequate sleep, and relaxation techniques like yoga or aromatherapy all contribute to healing emotional wounds. When you nurture your body, you're sending a message to yourself that you are worthy of care and attention.

Seeking Professional Help

Healing emotional wounds is often a process that cannot be done alone. **Seeking professional help** from a therapist or counselor can be an invaluable part of the healing journey, especially for empaths who may struggle to work through their emotions on their own.

When to Seek Therapy

It can be difficult for empaths to know when it's time to seek therapy. Empaths are often highly self-aware and may believe that they should be able to heal on their own. However, there are clear signs that therapy is necessary, including:

- **Constantly feeling overwhelmed by emotions**: If you find that your emotions are all-consuming and you are unable to find balance, therapy can help you gain emotional control and develop coping strategies.

- **Recurring patterns of unhealthy relationships**: If you continue to attract toxic individuals or find yourself stuck in the same painful dynamics, therapy can help you break those patterns and learn to establish healthier boundaries.

- **Feeling emotionally numb**: If you feel disconnected from your own emotions, unable to cry or express how you feel, it may be a sign that you have repressed too much emotional pain, and professional support can help you process it.

- **Trauma that won't go away**: If past trauma continues to haunt you and negatively impacts your daily life, seeking therapy can help you process and heal from these wounds.

Types of Therapy for Empaths

There are several types of therapy that can be particularly beneficial for empaths:

1. **Trauma-Informed Therapy**: This approach recognizes that trauma impacts both the mind and body, and focuses on creating a safe, supportive environment for healing. Trauma-informed therapy is gentle, and it allows the

empath to heal at their own pace without feeling rushed or pressured.

2. **Cognitive Behavioral Therapy (CBT)**: CBT is effective for breaking negative thought patterns and replacing them with healthier, more adaptive beliefs. For empaths dealing with self-blame, guilt, or shame, CBT can be incredibly powerful in reframing those negative thought patterns.

3. **Somatic Therapy**: Somatic therapy focuses on the mind-body connection and helps release trapped emotions from the body. Empaths who have stored trauma in their bodies may find somatic practices helpful in releasing those emotions and regaining a sense of emotional equilibrium.

4. **Energy Healing Therapies**: Energy-based therapies such as Reiki or acupuncture can support empaths in balancing their energy and healing from emotional wounds. These therapies focus on restoring the natural flow

of energy within the body and may complement traditional therapy practices.

5. **Group Therapy**: Group therapy provides a supportive community where empaths can share their experiences and learn from others who have gone through similar challenges. Group therapy helps build a sense of connection and reminds empaths that they are not alone in their journey.

Conclusion

Healing from emotional wounds is an ongoing journey that requires patience, perseverance, and self-compassion. For empaths, the process is often more intricate due to their sensitivity to others' emotions and the tendency to internalize pain. By acknowledging your pain, releasing self-blame and shame, practicing self-compassion, and seeking professional help when needed, you can begin to heal from your emotional wounds. Healing doesn't mean forgetting the past; it means learning to live in the present with a renewed sense of self-worth, clarity, and resilience. The path may be challenging, but the reward is a life that is richer, more fulfilling, and emotionally balanced.

Chapter 4 Takeaways

Acknowledging Your Pain: Accepting and acknowledging past trauma is the first step in healing, allowing an empath to confront their emotional wounds.

Moving Past Self-Blame and Shame: Healing requires releasing feelings of guilt and recognizing that the responsibility for abuse lies with the abuser, not the empath.

Practicing Self-Compassion: Building self-esteem and self-compassion helps empaths to heal and reconnect with their worth.

Affirmations and Mindfulness Practices: Positive affirmations and mindfulness techniques are tools that help empaths rebuild their self-esteem and process their emotional pain.

Seeking Professional Help: Therapy, particularly trauma-informed therapy, is a key resource for helping empaths heal from emotional abuse.

Types of Therapy: Different therapeutic approaches, such as cognitive-behavioral therapy (CBT) and mindfulness-based therapy, are effective in helping empaths process trauma and develop healthier emotional patterns.

Real-Life Applications

Acknowledging Pain

- **Prompt:** Write a letter to your past self, acknowledging the pain you've endured and offering compassion.

- **Example:**

  - Letter to self:

    "Dear Past Me,
    You've endured so much pain,
    especially from people who should
    have cared for you. I'm proud of how
    strong you've remained. Moving
    forward, I promise to protect you and
    prioritize your well-being."

Chapter 5: Strengthening Your Inner Core

Discovering Your True Self

The journey of strengthening your inner core begins with discovering who you truly are. It's about peeling back the layers of expectations, past trauma, and external influence to reconnect with your authentic self. For empaths, this process can be especially challenging, as you may have spent much of your life prioritizing others' feelings and needs, losing sight of your own desires and essence. Discovering your true self is the cornerstone of emotional empowerment, as it allows you to differentiate your needs, assert yourself, and establish boundaries that serve your well-being.

Differentiating Your Needs from Others'

Empaths often struggle to distinguish between their own needs and the emotional needs of others. This phenomenon occurs because empaths are naturally attuned to the feelings of those around them. They often absorb others' emotions, and over time, this can blur the lines between who they are and what they feel. If this goes unchecked, an empath may begin to neglect their own emotional needs or even lose their sense of self.

The first step in differentiating your needs from others' is **self-awareness**. This requires practicing mindfulness and paying close attention to your emotional state in different situations. It also requires asking yourself honest questions: "What am I truly feeling right now? Is this my emotion, or am I absorbing someone else's energy?" You may find that you're often catering to the needs of others, constantly reacting to external stimuli, rather than recognizing and addressing your own feelings.

To start differentiating between your needs and the emotions of others, try these strategies:

- **Check-In With Yourself Regularly**: Set aside time daily to check in with your emotions. This could be through journaling, meditation, or a few moments of quiet reflection. Write down how you're feeling and why you think you feel that way. Doing this will help you recognize patterns and learn to distinguish between your own emotions and the influence of others.

- **Ask Yourself What You Need**: In each situation, pause and ask yourself: "What do I need right now?" This may be as simple as a moment of solitude, a conversation, or some form of physical relaxation. Reconnecting with your needs will help you break the cycle of emotional dependence on others.

- **Practice Emotional Detachment**: Detachment doesn't mean shutting yourself off emotionally, but learning to not absorb the emotions of others. If you find yourself feeling overwhelmed by someone else's feelings, take a step back and remind yourself that their emotions are theirs to process, not yours.

The Power of Self-Reflection

Self-reflection is a powerful tool that empaths can use to discover their true selves. It's an opportunity to gain clarity, examine patterns in your behavior, and understand the driving forces behind your emotions. Without self-reflection, empaths may end up living their lives based on others' expectations, without a clear sense of personal direction.

Self-reflection allows you to step out of the cycle of people-pleasing and emotional overextension, guiding you back to a space where you can prioritize your own values, needs, and desires. It helps you understand who you are at your core, separate from the emotional noise of the world.

To engage in self-reflection:

1. **Practice Journaling**: Journaling is one of the most effective tools for self-reflection. Take time each day to reflect on your emotions, experiences, and what is happening in your life. Write about what you are grateful for, what challenges you are facing, and what you need to change or improve. Through journaling, you can begin to recognize themes in your life and understand the choices you're making.

2. **Meditative Practices**: Meditation helps clear your mind, making room for inner clarity.

Regular meditation enables you to tap into your intuition, gaining insight into your true self. You can also use guided meditations specifically designed for empaths, which focus on grounding your energy and connecting with your authentic self.

3. **Seek Feedback from Trusted Sources**: Sometimes, discovering who we truly are requires external perspectives. Ask close friends or family members about the qualities they see in you. Their insights can serve as valuable mirrors to help you gain a clearer view of your strengths, passions, and areas for growth.

Building Emotional Resilience

Once you've begun to reconnect with your true self, the next phase of strengthening your inner core involves developing emotional resilience. Life inevitably brings challenges, and as an empath, you may feel deeply impacted by them. Whether it's facing emotional turmoil from others or dealing with personal stress, emotional resilience helps you bounce back from difficulties without losing your sense of self.

Building resilience doesn't mean avoiding stress or pretending that you don't feel the weight of life's hardships. Instead, it's about learning to **adapt and grow** through adversity, so you can face life's challenges with strength, flexibility, and a sense of emotional balance.

Coping Mechanisms for High-Stress Situations

Stress is an inevitable part of life, and empaths may feel its effects more acutely than others. However, developing effective coping strategies allows you to manage stress in a way that supports your emotional health.

Here are some coping mechanisms that can help you manage stress:

1. **Breathing Exercises**: When you feel overwhelmed or anxious, focusing on your breath can help calm your mind and body. Try the box-breathing technique: inhale for a count of four, hold for four, exhale for four,

and hold for four. This rhythmic breathing can help slow your heart rate and activate your body's relaxation response.

2. **Mindfulness Practice**: Being present in the moment can greatly reduce stress. Practice mindfulness by focusing on your senses—what you can see, feel, hear, and smell. This will bring you back to the here and now, helping you distance yourself from emotional chaos.

3. **Grounding Exercises**: If you feel like you're overwhelmed by someone else's energy or emotions, grounding techniques can help you reconnect with yourself. Try standing with your feet firmly planted on the ground, imagining roots extending from the soles of your feet into the earth. This visualization helps you regain your balance and protect yourself from emotional overwhelm.

4. **Regular Exercise**: Physical movement has profound mental health benefits. Exercise releases endorphins, which are natural mood

boosters, while also helping to release any pent-up energy or tension from your body. Whether it's yoga, running, or simply walking, physical activity can help release emotional buildup and create a sense of emotional equilibrium.

5. **Emotional Expression**: Bottling up emotions often leads to emotional burnout. Allow yourself to express your emotions in a healthy way. This can be through journaling, art, dancing, or talking with a trusted friend. When you express your emotions, you are acknowledging them, which is an important step in building resilience.

6. **Spending Time in Nature**: Nature has a calming effect on the nervous system. Spend time outdoors, whether it's walking in a park, hiking in the mountains, or simply sitting by the ocean. Nature has a grounding, restorative effect that helps you reconnect with your inner peace.

Reframing Challenges as Growth Opportunities

One of the most powerful ways to build emotional resilience is to reframe challenges as opportunities for growth. Challenges are inevitable, but they are also an essential part of personal development. How you choose to respond to challenges greatly influences your ability to navigate them and emerge stronger.

Reframing challenges doesn't mean denying that they're difficult or painful. It means recognizing that challenges are an opportunity for growth, learning, and personal evolution. When you face adversity, ask yourself, "What can I learn from this?" or "How can this challenge help me grow?" Even if the situation feels overwhelmingly negative, there's often a lesson or strength to be found in the experience.

To practice reframing, consider these strategies:

- **View Challenges as Opportunities**: When facing a difficult situation, instead of focusing on the negative, ask yourself, "What strengths am I tapping into right now?" or "How can I use this situation to develop a new skill?"

Viewing challenges as opportunities for self-improvement helps you stay focused on the bigger picture.

- **Focus on the Process, Not Just the Outcome**: The journey is often more valuable than the destination. When faced with challenges, embrace the process of overcoming them, even if the outcome isn't exactly what you expected. The skills and wisdom you gain along the way are invaluable.

- **Practice Gratitude**: Even in difficult times, there is always something to be grateful for. Practicing gratitude helps shift your focus from what's lacking or painful to what is good in your life. It can bring perspective to challenging situations and provide emotional strength.

Practicing Assertiveness

Assertiveness is an essential tool for building your inner core. For empaths, who are often sensitive to the needs of others, learning to assert themselves without guilt is a powerful way to maintain healthy boundaries and emotional well-being. Assertiveness involves expressing your needs, desires, and boundaries in a direct and respectful way, without aggression or passivity.

For empaths, assertiveness isn't just about expressing your opinions—it's also about protecting your emotional energy and learning to say "no" when necessary.

Tools to Express Yourself Without Aggression

Assertiveness involves striking a balance between being passive and being aggressive. It's about expressing yourself confidently and clearly, without feeling the need to apologize for your needs. Here are some tools to express yourself assertively without aggression:

1. **Use "I" Statements**: The best way to express your emotions without sounding accusatory or blaming others is through "I" statements. For example, instead of saying, "You never listen to me," say, "I feel unheard when I don't receive a response." This takes the focus off

the other person and centers the conversation on your feelings.

2. **Practice Active Listening**: Assertiveness isn't just about speaking your truth—it's also about listening to others. By actively listening, you show respect for the other person's feelings and needs while maintaining your own boundaries.

3. **Calm Body Language**: When you express yourself assertively, your body language should reflect your calm, confident demeanor. Stand tall, make eye contact, and use open gestures. This will reinforce your message and show that you're firm but respectful.

The Art of Saying "No" Confidently

Saying "no" is one of the most difficult yet crucial skills for empaths to master. Saying "no" without guilt or hesitation is a form of emotional self-care and a crucial part of setting healthy boundaries. Here's how to say "no" confidently:

1. **Be Clear and Firm**: When you say "no," make sure it's clear and without wavering. Avoid the temptation to explain or justify your decision too much. Simply say, "No, I'm unable to do that" or "No, I cannot commit to that right now."

2. **Practice Self-Care After Saying "No"**: Saying "no" can sometimes feel uncomfortable or even guilt-inducing. Afterward, practice self-care to reinforce the choice you made. Engage in an activity that reaffirms your decision, such as taking a walk, meditating, or spending time with loved ones.

3. **Embrace the Power of Boundaries**: Remember that setting boundaries is an act of self-respect. When you say "no," you're protecting your time, energy, and emotional well-being. By saying "no," you're saying "yes" to your own needs and priorities.

Conclusion

Strengthening your inner core as an empath requires a deep commitment to self-discovery, emotional resilience, and assertiveness. As you reconnect with your true self and prioritize your own needs, you can build the foundation for a life of emotional balance and well-being. By differentiating your emotions from those of others, engaging in self-reflection, developing resilience, and practicing assertiveness, you can cultivate a sense of inner strength that empowers you to navigate the challenges of life with confidence.

Empathy is a powerful gift, but it's only through self-awareness and self-care that you can fully embrace it without losing yourself. Strengthening your inner core isn't just about surviving; it's about thriving in a world that needs your light and your authenticity.

Chapter 5 Takeaways

Discovering Your True Self: Self-reflection helps empaths reconnect with their authentic self, separate from the influence of narcissistic relationships.

Differentiating Your Needs from Others': Understanding the difference between personal needs and the needs of others allows empaths to prioritize their own well-being.

The Power of Self-Reflection: Self-reflection helps to clarify goals, values, and emotional needs, and can act as a powerful tool in healing.

Building Emotional Resilience: Coping mechanisms, such as mindfulness, exercise, and self-compassion, are crucial for managing stress and building resilience in the face of emotional challenges.

Reframing Challenges as Growth Opportunities: Viewing challenges as opportunities for growth helps empaths see adversity as part of the healing process.

Practicing Assertiveness: Assertiveness techniques allow empaths to express themselves without aggression, ensuring that their needs are communicated in healthy ways.

The Art of Saying "No" Confidently: Learning to say "no" with confidence and without guilt is essential to maintaining emotional health and self-preservation.

Real-Life Applications

Self-Reflection

- **Prompt:** Answer the question: "Who am I when I'm not taking care of others?" List your interests, dreams, and desires.

- **Example:**

  - o Answer: "I am a creative, thoughtful person who loves painting, writing, and spending time in nature. These are things I've neglected but want to prioritize again."

Chapter 6: Cultivating Healthy Relationships

Creating and sustaining healthy relationships is one of the most important practices for an empath's well-being. As an empath, you have the ability to deeply connect with others, understand their emotions, and offer profound support. However, this heightened sensitivity can sometimes lead to emotional drain and burnout if the relationships you engage in are not mutually beneficial or balanced. Cultivating healthy relationships, therefore, requires self-awareness, a firm understanding of boundaries, and the ability to choose people who respect your emotional needs. This chapter will explore what makes relationships healthy, how to select positive influences, and how to nourish these connections with care.

What Makes a Relationship Healthy?

A healthy relationship doesn't just happen; it is cultivated through effort, communication, and a shared understanding of needs and boundaries. Whether it is a romantic relationship, a close friendship, or a professional connection, the basic tenets of a healthy relationship are grounded in mutual respect, emotional safety, reciprocity, and authenticity. These aspects form the foundation for any successful relationship and allow for both individuals to flourish emotionally, mentally, and spiritually.

Reciprocity, Respect, and Authenticity

In a relationship, **reciprocity** is essential for balance. This means that both individuals contribute emotionally, mentally, or physically in a way that is mutually satisfying. For empaths, this can often be a tricky balance to strike because they tend to give more than they receive, often out of a deep-seated desire to help and support others. However, healthy relationships are based on the idea that both parties feel nurtured and fulfilled. Reciprocity in a relationship doesn't mean keeping score, but rather ensuring that each person feels valued, loved, and supported in a way that aligns with their needs.

- **Reciprocity** in an empath's relationships should involve emotional exchanges that make both individuals feel emotionally sustained. If you find that one person is continually taking emotional energy without giving anything back, it may be a sign that the relationship is out of balance. Healthy relationships should be a two-way street.

- **Respect** is perhaps the cornerstone of any successful relationship. It's about honoring each other's boundaries, emotions, and thoughts. For empaths, respect means having your sensitivity acknowledged and understood. A person who respects you will not push you past your limits or make you feel guilty for needing space or for expressing your emotions. Instead, they will create a safe environment for you to be yourself without fear of judgment.

- **Authenticity** is another important element of healthy relationships. To be authentic means to show up as your true self in the relationship without pretense or fear of rejection. In a healthy relationship, you feel free to express your thoughts, feelings, and needs as they are, without the need to change or suppress them for the sake of the other person's comfort. For empaths, this is crucial because being authentic allows you to protect your energy and assert your needs without compromise.

The Importance of Shared Values

In addition to the foundational components of reciprocity, respect, and authenticity, **shared values** play a vital role in determining the health of a relationship. Values are the guiding principles that shape the way you make decisions, how you behave, and how you relate to others. When two individuals share core values such as trust, honesty, kindness, or spiritual beliefs, it fosters a sense of mutual understanding and alignment.

- For empaths, shared values can create an emotional connection that runs deeper than surface-level interactions. For example, if you value compassion and kindness and you find someone who shares those values, it creates a natural bond. You will both understand that acts of kindness, whether big or small, are meaningful and impactful.

- **Shared values** can also ensure that you align in terms of long-term goals, such as family, career aspirations, and lifestyle. For example, in romantic relationships, compatibility in values like the importance of family, communication, and growth can serve as a strong foundation for a lasting bond.

It's important to note that shared values don't mean you agree on every single thing, but they provide a common thread that runs through the relationship and helps to foster trust, understanding, and mutual support.

Choosing the Right People

As an empath, choosing the right people to surround yourself with is one of the most crucial aspects of cultivating healthy relationships. You are naturally drawn to people who are emotionally expressive or who seem to need your help and support. While these individuals may seem like they need you, and you may feel compelled to nurture them, it's essential to ensure that these relationships are balanced and do not drain you. Choosing the right people involves recognizing the traits that contribute to a healthy, supportive connection while avoiding those who may be toxic or emotionally draining.

Recognizing Kindred Spirits and Positive Influences

Kindred spirits are people with whom you feel a deep emotional connection. These are the people who understand you on a level that goes beyond words and who offer love, understanding, and compassion without expectation or judgment. Kindred spirits come in many forms—close friends, romantic partners, family members, or even mentors. For empaths, these relationships are invaluable because they offer emotional nourishment and a sense of deep connection.

- **Energy Alignment**: Kindred spirits often share an energy resonance with you. When you are in their presence, you feel seen, heard, and understood. There is no need to perform or put up a facade. The relationship feels effortless because there is a natural understanding of one another's emotional needs.

- **Non-judgmental Acceptance**: These individuals accept you for who you are, flaws and all. They do not try to change you or expect you to fit a mold. For empaths, this type of acceptance is essential because it allows you to show up as your authentic self without fear of rejection.

- **Shared Growth**: Kindred spirits support your personal growth and encourage you to evolve. These relationships do not stagnate; instead, they challenge you to become the best version of yourself while offering unconditional love and support.

Recognizing kindred spirits involves paying attention to how you feel when you interact with someone. If being around them feels like a safe, nurturing space that allows you to be yourself, you've likely found a kindred spirit.

Avoiding Relationships Rooted in Dependency

While some relationships are deeply nourishing, others may be built on **dependency**—where one person relies heavily on the other for emotional, physical, or psychological support. This can be an unhealthy dynamic, especially for empaths, as it often leads to an imbalance where the empath gives endlessly without receiving anything in return.

Signs of dependency in a relationship include:

- **One-Sided Emotional Labor**: You may find that you are always the one who provides emotional support, advice, or comfort while the other person rarely reciprocates or acknowledges your emotional needs.

- **Unclear Boundaries**: The other person may have difficulty respecting your boundaries, whether it's demanding your time or expecting emotional labor without regard for your own needs.

- **Imbalance in Power**: In a dependent relationship, one person may dominate or control the relationship, often making decisions for both individuals without consulting the other or disregarding their needs.

- **Lack of Independence**: In a codependent relationship, the other person may lack the emotional resilience to function independently and may rely on you excessively for validation, decision-making, or emotional regulation.

To avoid these types of relationships, it's crucial to establish and maintain strong boundaries and to recognize when someone is taking more than they are giving. Trust your intuition; if you feel drained, unappreciated, or emotionally manipulated, it may be time to reevaluate the relationship. Being an empath doesn't mean sacrificing your well-being for others— it means offering your compassion in a way that is balanced, healthy, and sustainable.

Nurturing Relationships with Care

Once you've established healthy relationships, it's important to nurture them with care and intention. Nurturing relationships with care involves being present, offering emotional support, and giving love, but it also requires making sure that you are not overextending yourself or neglecting your own emotional needs.

How to Give Without Overextending Yourself

Empaths often feel a strong sense of responsibility to care for others, but this can lead to emotional burnout if not managed properly. It's important to learn how to give without overextending yourself, ensuring that your emotional reserves remain replenished.

To give without overextending:

- **Recognize Your Limits**: Pay attention to how you feel during and after interactions with others. If you start feeling drained or overwhelmed, it's a sign that you may have reached your emotional limit. It's okay to take a step back and recharge.

- **Set Boundaries**: Establish clear boundaries around your time, energy, and emotional availability. For example, if a friend needs emotional support, but you've had a long, draining day, it's okay to say, "I'm happy to talk tomorrow, but I need some time to rest tonight."

- **Ask for Reciprocation**: It's important to be able to ask for what you need in return. If you are constantly giving emotional support to others, don't be afraid to ask for support in return. This could mean asking a friend for advice or simply needing someone to listen to you.

Balancing Empathy with Self-Preservation

Empathy is a gift, but without proper self-preservation, it can quickly become a burden. As an empath, it's essential to protect your emotional energy while still being compassionate and caring for others.

To balance empathy with self-preservation:

- **Practice Emotional Detachment**: Emotional detachment doesn't mean being cold or unfeeling; it means recognizing that the emotions of others are not yours to carry. When you find yourself absorbing someone else's emotions, take a step back and remind yourself that their feelings are their own. Use grounding techniques, such as deep breathing or visualization, to release their emotional energy from your body.

- **Engage in Self-Care**: Make self-care a priority. Take time each day to engage in activities that replenish your emotional energy, such as meditation, exercise, journaling, or spending time in nature. The more you care for yourself, the more you will be able to show up for others in a healthy, balanced way.

- **Learn to Say "No"**: Learning to say "no" is one of the most important aspects of self-preservation. Empaths often feel compelled to help others at the expense of their own well-being, but it's essential to recognize when you need to say "no" in order to protect your emotional health. Saying "no" is not selfish; it is an act of self-respect and a way to ensure that you have the energy to nurture relationships in a healthy way.

Conclusion

Cultivating healthy relationships as an empath involves a combination of self-awareness, strong boundaries, and the ability to recognize individuals who nourish and support you. By seeking relationships based on reciprocity, respect, and shared values, you create a foundation for mutual growth and understanding. Choosing the right people—kindred spirits who align with your energy and emotional needs—ensures that your emotional investments are well placed.

Nurturing these relationships with care and balancing empathy with self-preservation is essential for maintaining your emotional well-being. By practicing emotional detachment, setting clear boundaries, and prioritizing self-care, you can offer your support and love without sacrificing your own needs. Healthy relationships are not only about giving—they are about creating a space where both individuals can thrive.

Ultimately, when you invest in relationships that respect and uplift you, you create a circle of support that enables you to experience deep connection, joy, and fulfillment. Healthy relationships are the cornerstone of a vibrant, balanced life, and as an empath, they are key to maintaining your emotional resilience while sharing your gifts with the world.

Chapter 6 Takeaways

What Makes a Relationship Healthy?: Healthy relationships are built on reciprocity, respect, and authenticity, with both parties prioritizing each other's emotional well-being.

The Importance of Shared Values: Shared values and goals are the foundation for creating long-lasting, supportive relationships.

Choosing the Right People: Empaths should surround themselves with individuals who uplift and respect them, avoiding those who foster dependency or manipulation.

Avoiding Relationships Rooted in Dependency: Recognizing and avoiding relationships where one person is overly reliant on the other helps to maintain healthy emotional dynamics.

Nurturing Relationships with Care: Giving without overextending oneself requires balancing care for others with self-preservation.

Balancing Empathy with Self-Preservation: Empaths must learn to nurture relationships without compromising their own emotional needs and boundaries.

Real-Life Applications

Relationship Inventory

- **Prompt:** Categorize your relationships into three groups: uplifting, neutral, and draining. Decide which ones to nurture and which to reevaluate.

- **Example:**

    o Uplifting: My sister, close friend Sarah.

    o Neutral: Colleagues from work.

o   Draining: An old school friend who always complains and dismisses my concerns.

o   Action Plan: "I'll focus on spending more time with Sarah and creating boundaries with the draining friend."

Chapter 7: Detaching from Narcissistic Individuals

In the emotionally charged world of narcissistic relationships, detaching from a narcissist can be the most empowering yet heartbreaking experience of your life. Empaths, in particular, can find this journey exceptionally challenging because they tend to feel deeply connected to others' emotions and needs. Yet, when it comes to narcissistic relationships, these connections often foster manipulation, emotional depletion, and abuse. Understanding when and how to detach is essential not just for surviving but for ultimately thriving.

In this expanded chapter, we will further explore the process of detaching from a narcissist. We will delve deeper into recognizing the signs that you need to let go, the psychological and emotional impact of detachment, strategies for implementing the No-Contact Rule, and how to cope with the aftermath, including grief, guilt, and reclaiming your life. By the end of this chapter, you'll have a clear framework for leaving a toxic relationship behind while caring for your emotional health.

Recognizing When It's Time to Let Go

Understanding when it's time to leave a narcissistic relationship is a difficult yet crucial part of the healing process. Empaths often struggle to walk away because of their deep sense of empathy, attachment, and desire to help. However, staying in such relationships can prevent personal growth and lead to long-term emotional and psychological damage.

Patterns That Indicate Irreparable Harm

1. **Constant Emotional Turmoil**: Narcissistic individuals are known for creating a constant state of emotional chaos. The relationship may feel like a roller coaster where at one moment, you're the most important person in their life, and the next, you're invisible, devalued, or even vilified. Over time, this emotional rollercoaster drains you, leaving you feeling confused, frustrated, and emotionally numb.

2. **Isolation from Support Systems**: Narcissists often manipulate their victims by isolating them from friends, family, and other sources of support. They may subtly undermine your relationships, leaving you feeling alone and unsupported. Over time, you might begin to doubt the advice and perspectives of those who care about you, making it harder to recognize the toxic dynamics at play.

3. **A Pattern of Broken Promises and Empty Words**: Narcissists are masters at making grand promises they never intend to keep. They often promise change, but these promises are never fulfilled, leaving you in a constant state of hope followed by disappointment. This cycle of broken promises erodes your self-worth and hope for the relationship.

4. **Emotional Exhaustion and Burnout**: You may feel emotionally drained from constantly trying to meet the narcissist's needs, appease them, or navigate their volatile moods. Even when you do everything "right," nothing is

ever enough. This emotional burnout leaves you feeling incapable of healing or growing, further confirming that the relationship has become toxic.

5. **Feeling Like You're Walking on Eggshells**: Narcissists can create a climate of fear in which you feel constantly on edge, never knowing when the next outburst or emotional manipulation will happen. If you've started to avoid speaking your mind or expressing your feelings for fear of backlash, it's a clear sign that the relationship is emotionally unsafe.

6. **Overpowering Guilt**: Narcissists often use guilt as a tool of control. If you constantly feel guilty about needing time for yourself, having your own opinions, or asserting your boundaries, it's a sign that the relationship is unhealthy. Narcissists make you feel like a selfish person for wanting to meet your own needs, and over time, this guilt can cripple your self-esteem.

7. **The Relationship Is Draining Your Self-Worth**: Narcissists thrive on diminishing the self-worth of others to boost their own fragile egos. If you find that your self-esteem has eroded, that you no longer recognize yourself, or that you constantly feel like you are not enough, it's time to step back and reevaluate your relationship.

Recognizing these patterns is a form of self-awareness. It's the moment when you understand that, no matter how hard you try, the narcissist will never truly change. Accepting that you cannot fix them or save them is the first step to healing. It's a powerful acknowledgment that your emotional health is far more important than trying to salvage an abusive or unfulfilling relationship.

Emotional and Physical Safety Considerations

When detaching from a narcissist, emotional and physical safety are paramount. Narcissists can become volatile when they sense they are losing control over a person or relationship, so it's important to approach the detachment process with caution.

1. **Emotional Safety**: The emotional impact of leaving a narcissistic relationship can be profound. Narcissists often use emotional manipulation to keep you trapped, including guilt, fear, and shame. They may react with anger, sadness, or a desperate attempt to reignite the relationship, which can leave you feeling guilty or anxious. In the face of this, protecting your emotional safety means distancing yourself from the narcissist's emotional warfare. Do not engage in debates or attempts to explain yourself, as this can re-open old wounds and prolong the manipulation.

2. **Physical Safety**: If the relationship has become physically abusive or if you fear that the narcissist could harm you physically during the separation, you must prioritize your physical safety. Create a safety plan, which might involve contacting a support network, a therapist, or even local authorities. Remember

that leaving is the best way to ensure your physical and emotional well-being. Reach out to domestic violence hotlines or shelters for further support if needed.

The No-Contact Rule

The No-Contact Rule is an essential tool for anyone detaching from a narcissistic relationship. The act of severing all ties with a narcissist is necessary for the healing process and for preventing further manipulation. When applied effectively, the No-Contact Rule helps to reclaim your sense of self and protects you from continued emotional abuse.

Why the No-Contact Rule Works

The No-Contact Rule works for several reasons:

1. **Prevents Further Manipulation**: Narcissists thrive on being able to manipulate their victims. By cutting off all communication, you remove their ability to continue feeding off your energy, emotions, and responses. Every time you respond to them, even with anger or frustration, you give them power over you. The No-Contact Rule takes that power away

and breaks the cycle of emotional manipulation.

2. **Emotional Healing**: The space created by no contact allows you to start the healing process. You are no longer exposed to the toxic behavior, enabling your emotions to reset. This space gives you the clarity and mental peace needed to process your emotions, establish healthy boundaries, and regain a sense of control.

3. **Establishes Firm Boundaries**: Narcissists have a knack for crossing boundaries and using emotional blackmail to make you feel responsible for their feelings. The No-Contact Rule enforces a boundary that cannot be crossed, signaling that you are no longer available to be manipulated or controlled.

4. **Prevents Hoovering**: Narcissists often employ a tactic called "hoovering," where they try to suck you back into the relationship using charm, guilt, or promises of change. By going No-Contact, you prevent the narcissist from

using these tactics to lure you back into their emotional web.

How to Implement the No-Contact Rule

1. **Prepare Yourself Emotionally**: Before cutting all ties, it's essential to prepare yourself emotionally. Recognize that you may experience feelings of guilt, loneliness, or even doubt about your decision. These emotions are part of the process, but they are not indications that you made the wrong choice.

2. **Block All Communication**: Block the narcissist on all platforms—phone, email, social media, messaging apps, and any other ways they might contact you. Narcissists may try to contact you through mutual friends or family members, so it's important to communicate with them about your decision and ask them to respect your wishes for no contact.

3. **Limit Access to Shared Spaces**: If you live with the narcissist or have shared spaces (workplace, mutual friends), take measures to

limit contact. You may need to find alternative living arrangements, change your daily routine, or modify your social circle temporarily to avoid interacting with the narcissist.

4. **Stay Firm and Stay No-Contact**: This is the hardest part. Narcissists are skilled at convincing others to re-engage with them. They may send guilt-laden messages, apologize (insincerely), or promise to change. However, stay firm and do not respond. The moment you re-engage, you risk falling back into the manipulation cycle.

5. **Get Support**: Cutting off a narcissist can feel lonely and isolating, but you don't have to do it alone. Seek support from friends, family, or therapists who understand what you're going through. Support groups for narcissistic abuse survivors can also offer valuable insight and encouragement as you move through the detachment process.

Coping with the Aftermath

Once you've detached from the narcissist, the emotional fallout may take time to heal. The damage done by narcissistic abuse often runs deep, and it's crucial to allow yourself to grieve, heal, and find closure on your own terms.

Managing Guilt, Grief, and Closure

1. **Managing Guilt**: Guilt is a powerful and pervasive emotion, especially for empaths who often feel responsible for others. After leaving a narcissist, you may feel guilty for "hurting" them, for abandoning them in their time of need, or for not being able to fix them. Remember, this guilt is manipulation. The narcissist has trained you to believe that their needs come first. It's vital to remind yourself that you did not abandon them—you chose yourself and your well-being.

2. **Dealing with Grief**: Even when a relationship is toxic, there may be moments of love and care that you grieve. It's important to honor that grief without romanticizing the

relationship or falling into nostalgia. Understand that grieving the loss of the relationship is part of the healing process, but also remind yourself of the reasons why you left. Embrace the grieving process, but allow it to eventually lead you to acceptance and healing.

3. **Finding Closure**: Narcissists rarely provide closure. They often gaslight, blame-shift, or dismiss your feelings when you seek closure. This is why it's crucial to find your own closure. This might involve writing a letter to the narcissist that you never send, reflecting on what the relationship taught you, or simply acknowledging that the relationship was never going to meet your needs. Closure is not about receiving answers—it's about making peace with the fact that the relationship was toxic and no longer serves you.

Finding Joy in Newfound Freedom

After detaching from a narcissist, you will begin the process of reclaiming your life. While the road may seem daunting, there is immense freedom to be found in taking back control over your own life and happiness.

1. **Rediscover Your Passions**: Narcissistic relationships often cause you to lose sight of your own needs and desires. Take time to rediscover your passions and interests— whether it's a creative pursuit, traveling, or simply spending time with loved ones. This time for self-reflection and self-discovery will help you reconnect with the person you were before the narcissist's influence.

2. **Cultivate Healthy Relationships**: Surround yourself with people who truly care for you and who reciprocate your energy and empathy. Healthy relationships are built on mutual respect, trust, and love. The joy of interacting with individuals who value you and who don't drain your emotional energy is

one of the greatest rewards of detaching from narcissistic individuals.

3. **Healing and Personal Growth**: Detaching from a narcissist often catalyzes personal growth. You'll learn to set firmer boundaries, develop a deeper understanding of your own emotional needs, and cultivate resilience. Personal healing is a lifelong process, but every step forward helps you become stronger, wiser, and more connected to your authentic self.

4. **Reclaim Your Self-Worth**: Narcissistic abuse often strips away your self-esteem. Through self-compassion, therapy, and mindfulness, you can rebuild your sense of self-worth. Remind yourself that you are deserving of love, respect, and kindness, and take steps to nurture yourself emotionally, mentally, and physically.

Conclusion

Detaching from a narcissistic individual is a difficult yet life-changing decision. It requires immense courage, self-compassion, and a commitment to your emotional well-being. The process involves recognizing the toxic patterns in the relationship, implementing strategies like the No-Contact Rule, and coping with the emotional fallout. Most importantly, it opens the door to healing, self-empowerment, and a future filled with healthy, fulfilling relationships.

The journey may be long, but each step you take away from the narcissist brings you closer to the most important relationship you'll ever have: the one with yourself. It's time to embrace your freedom, trust in your inner strength, and begin the process of rediscovering the joy and peace that you deserve.

Chapter 7 Takeaways

Recognizing When It's Time to Let Go: Emotional and physical safety should always come first;

knowing when to walk away from a toxic relationship is vital.

Patterns of Irreparable Harm: Recognizing patterns such as constant emotional manipulation, disregard for boundaries, and lack of empathy as signs that a relationship is no longer healthy.

The No-Contact Rule: Implementing no contact can help an empath break free from the emotional entanglement of narcissistic abuse, providing time and space for healing.

Alternatives if Full Detachment Isn't Possible: In some cases, a full break may not be possible (e.g., shared children), but limiting contact and setting firm boundaries can still provide significant emotional relief.

Coping with the Aftermath: The aftermath of detaching from a narcissist involves managing feelings of guilt, grief, and the process of finding closure.

Finding Joy in Newfound Freedom: Embracing the freedom that comes with detachment can bring newfound joy, peace, and personal growth.

Real-Life Applications

Evaluating Relationships

- **Prompt:** List the pros and cons of staying connected to a toxic individual. Use this to guide your decision about detachment.

- **Example:**

  - Pros of staying connected: Familiarity, shared memories.

  - Cons of staying connected: Emotional manipulation, constant criticism, feeling unworthy.

  - **Reflection:** "The cons clearly outweigh the pros. It's time to detach and prioritize my mental health."

Chapter 8: Rediscovering Joy and Purpose

Reconnecting with Your Passions

For many empaths recovering from narcissistic relationships, one of the most profound sources of healing comes from reconnecting with passions, hobbies, and desires that might have been buried or dismissed while in the toxic relationship. Narcissistic relationships often involve emotional manipulation, control, and a subtle erasure of one's sense of self. Your identity becomes entangled with the narcissist's needs, and over time, you may lose sight of your personal interests or aspirations. Reconnecting with your passions is an essential part of the healing journey, allowing you to rebuild a solid sense of self and return to a state of emotional equilibrium.

How Creativity Can Heal Emotional Wounds

Creativity is an especially powerful tool for healing emotional wounds. When you engage in creative activities, you express emotions, thoughts, and energy that may have been suppressed or distorted during the time spent in a toxic relationship. For empaths who are naturally attuned to the emotions and energies of others, creativity provides a safe space for releasing and processing these emotions without feeling overwhelmed by them.

1. **Creative Expression as Emotional Release** Narcissistic relationships can often lead to a situation where you suppress your feelings to keep the peace or avoid confrontation. The act of creating something—whether through writing, painting, playing an instrument, or crafting—serves as a conduit for your emotions. Creative outlets allow you to externalize and process your internal world in a tangible way. For example, writing in a journal or through poetry can be incredibly cathartic, providing a safe space to articulate feelings of confusion, anger, sadness, or

betrayal that might be hard to express verbally.

2. **The Flow State as Emotional Healing**

   Engaging in creative activities can put you in a state of "flow," where you are fully immersed in the activity and detached from external distractions. The flow state provides a deep sense of calm and focus, which is essential for emotional healing. During this time, you may find that past emotional pain or trauma fades into the background, allowing your body and mind to focus entirely on the present moment. This not only helps with the emotional release but also offers a reprieve from the inner chaos that comes with healing from narcissistic abuse.

3. **Vulnerability and Reclaiming Your Authentic Self**

   One of the most healing aspects of creativity is that it encourages vulnerability. Narcissistic abuse often forces you to hide or deny your authentic self in order to maintain the relationship. The act of creating something with no expectation of external validation opens the door to self-acceptance. Art, music, or writing, for instance, can be deeply personal and a means of reclaiming your true identity. Being vulnerable in your creative expression allows you to reconnect with the person you were before the toxic relationship —and the person you will become as you heal.

Activities That Bring Fulfillment and Peace

Beyond creative pursuits, there are numerous activities and practices that can help you rediscover fulfillment and peace. These activities are powerful tools to reconnect with your inner joy and sense of purpose.

1. **Physical Activity: Rebuilding Your Strength**
   Physical exercise is not only beneficial for your body but also for your mind. The mind-body connection is crucial during emotional recovery, and physical activity helps to restore balance. Exercise reduces cortisol (the stress hormone) and increases endorphins, which

are chemicals in the brain responsible for feelings of happiness. Whether you engage in yoga, running, swimming, or even a simple walk in the park, physical activity is essential for emotional healing. For empaths, exercise is a grounding practice that reconnects you with your body. Narcissistic relationships can often leave you feeling disconnected from yourself, and engaging in mindful movement can be a key tool in restoring that connection. Gentle activities like yoga or Tai Chi can also help you to manage stress, release negative energy, and regain a sense of control over your body and emotions.

2. **Spending Time in Nature: Restoring Balance**
   The natural world has a profound healing effect on the human psyche. Studies show that spending time outdoors can reduce stress, lower blood pressure, and improve mental clarity. Nature's inherent beauty and rhythm offer an antidote to the chaos and confusion of a toxic relationship. For empaths who are

sensitive to the emotions and energies around them, nature provides a neutral environment that allows you to reconnect with your own energy without being influenced by external negativity.

Simple activities like walking in a forest, sitting by the ocean, or hiking in the mountains can foster peace and renewal. Nature serves as a reminder that life continues to flow, that there is beauty and stillness beyond the noise of human conflict. As you immerse yourself in nature, allow yourself to feel its rejuvenating energy. Let the wind, the trees, and the earth support your healing process.

3. **Mindfulness and Meditation: Rebuilding Your Inner   Peace**

Mindfulness and meditation offer an invaluable opportunity to slow down and reconnect with yourself. After years of living in the emotional turmoil of a narcissistic relationship, developing a consistent mindfulness practice can help you find peace amidst chaos. Mindfulness involves being present in the moment and observing your thoughts and feelings without judgment. Meditation, on the other hand, is a way to quiet the mind and cultivate inner stillness. One of the most important things to practice is the idea of "self-compassion" during your meditation. Instead of berating yourself for having negative feelings or intrusive thoughts, treat yourself with kindness and understanding. Meditation can become a powerful anchor during the healing process, especially if you incorporate gratitude practices into your routine.

4. **Volunteering and Acts of Kindness: Creating Meaningful Connections**

   Helping others is not only beneficial for those you assist but can also bring a sense of meaning and fulfillment to your life. Volunteering allows you to step outside of your own experience and connect with a wider community. Acts of kindness, whether large or small, create a ripple effect that extends beyond you. As you step into the role of a giver rather than someone who is constantly giving to others, you can regain a sense of self-worth and confidence. Volunteering also helps to shift the focus from your pain to something larger than yourself. It can be a means of rebuilding trust in humanity and forming healthy connections with others. Giving without expecting anything in return fosters a deep sense of purpose and joy.

Practicing Gratitude

Gratitude is a potent tool for shifting your mindset, especially after the deep emotional wounds of narcissistic abuse. It is easy to feel as though everything has been taken from you, but cultivating a gratitude practice helps you to recognize the abundance in your life and opens your heart to healing.

How Gratitude Shifts Your Mindset

When you engage in regular gratitude practices, you change the way your brain perceives the world. Instead of focusing on the things that went wrong, gratitude redirects your focus to the things that are going right, no matter how small. Gratitude rewires the brain's neural pathways, enhancing your emotional resilience and helping you stay grounded in positive thoughts.

1. **Rewiring the Brain**
   Research has shown that gratitude activates the brain's reward centers and promotes the release of dopamine and serotonin, both of which are associated with positive emotions. By making gratitude a habit, you begin to rewire your brain to automatically seek out the good in your life. This is especially valuable after narcissistic abuse, where your self-worth may have been eroded by constant emotional manipulation.

2. **Shifting from Scarcity to Abundance**
   Narcissistic abuse often fosters a sense of

scarcity—feeling like you're not enough or that there's never enough love, attention, or validation to go around. Gratitude helps you shift from this scarcity mindset to an abundance mindset. It trains you to recognize the many blessings in your life, whether they are big or small, and to appreciate them fully.

3. **Building Emotional Resilience**
The practice of gratitude builds emotional resilience by teaching you to focus on your internal strengths rather than external circumstances. It helps you recognize that you are capable of moving forward and finding joy despite the pain. With a strong foundation of gratitude, you are better equipped to navigate the ups and downs of life after narcissistic abuse.

Daily Practices for a Positive Outlook

Integrating gratitude into your daily routine doesn't require a huge time commitment—it's the small, consistent practices that yield the most significant results over time.

1. **Gratitude Journaling**

    Spend a few minutes each day writing down three to five things you are grateful for. These can range from simple things like a warm cup of tea or a moment of peace to more profound things, such as a supportive friend or your ability to take steps toward healing. Writing them down makes them tangible and reinforces a positive mindset.

2. **Gratitude Meditation**

    During your meditation sessions, take time to focus on the things you are grateful for. Visualize each blessing, whether it's your health, your home, or your ability to take care of yourself. The more specific you can be, the more powerful the practice becomes.

3. **Gratitude Reminders**

    Place visual reminders of your blessings around your home or workspace. A photo of a loved one, a quote, or a simple object that represents something you are grateful for can serve as a quick, visual cue to shift your focus toward the positive aspects of your life when you're feeling overwhelmed.

4. **Gratitude Rituals**

    Consider creating a daily gratitude ritual, where you take a few moments before bed or first thing in the morning to acknowledge the good things in your life. This simple practice can significantly enhance your mood and help you sleep better at night.

Living Authentically

One of the greatest gifts you can give yourself after a toxic relationship is the permission to live authentically. Narcissistic abuse often forces you to suppress your true desires, emotions, and values in order to accommodate the narcissist's needs. The process of healing and rediscovering joy involves shedding these layers of inauthenticity and returning to the core of who you are.

Letting Go of Societal Expectations

We live in a society that often imposes rigid expectations on how we should behave, look, or live. These external pressures can weigh heavily on empaths, who are naturally sensitive to the opinions and judgments of others. To live authentically, you must let go of these societal expectations and embrace the truth of who you are, even if it doesn't align with conventional norms.

1. **Challenging Social Conditioning**

   Throughout our lives, we are conditioned to meet certain standards of success and happiness, often influenced by family, culture, and social media. However, living authentically requires you to question these societal norms and assess whether they truly align with your values and desires. You do not need to conform to others' expectations to feel worthy. Your worth is inherent in who you are.

2. **Redefining Success**

   In a world that equates success with material wealth, power, or status, redefining success is an act of reclaiming your individuality. For you, success might mean living a balanced life, nurturing meaningful relationships, or pursuing personal growth. It's important to define success on your own terms and release the need for validation from others.

Embracing Your Unique Path

Living authentically means embracing your unique journey, with all its twists and turns. No one else has lived your experiences, and no one else can walk your path. The process of rediscovering joy is about embracing your individuality and celebrating what makes you, *you.*

1. **Trusting Your Inner Compass**

    After narcissistic abuse, it's easy to feel disconnected from your intuition. But your inner voice has always been there, guiding you toward what is best for you. Take time to listen to your gut and trust the feelings that arise. Your intuition is the key to living authentically, helping you make decisions that honor your true self.

2. **Letting Go of Comparisons**

    One of the most destructive habits after a narcissistic relationship is comparing yourself to others. The narcissist often thrives on creating feelings of inadequacy, making you believe that you don't measure up. It's crucial to stop comparing your journey to anyone else's. Your path is unique, and your healing is personal.

3. **Living with Intention**

   Authentic living requires intentionality. Set meaningful goals that align with your passions, values, and vision for the future. Every small action taken with purpose brings you closer to your true self and deeper fulfillment. These intentional steps, however small, gradually build a life that reflects your authentic desires and aspirations.

Conclusion

Rediscovering joy and purpose after narcissistic abuse is not an overnight process. It is a journey that requires patience, self-compassion, and courage. But through reconnecting with your passions, practicing gratitude, and living authentically, you are creating the foundation for a life that reflects who you truly are. This chapter offers you tools to reclaim your emotional and spiritual well-being, to rediscover the joy that was lost, and to live with intention and purpose.

Healing from narcissistic abuse involves more than just surviving; it involves thriving and rediscovering the beauty of life. Through creativity, gratitude, and authenticity, you have the power to rebuild a life that is meaningful, fulfilling, and uniquely yours. By embracing your passions, appreciating life's small blessings, and honoring your true self, you will find that joy and purpose are not just possible—they are waiting for you to embrace them.

Chapter 8 Takeaways

Reconnecting with Your Passions: Rediscovering activities that bring fulfillment and peace can help empaths regain their sense of self and purpose after leaving toxic relationships.

How Creativity Can Heal Emotional Wounds: Creative expression offers a way to release and process emotions, providing healing through artistic outlets.

Practicing Gratitude: Gratitude helps shift the focus from what was lost to what remains, fostering a positive mindset.

Daily Practices for a Positive Outlook: Establishing daily practices, such as journaling or mindfulness, can help empaths maintain a balanced and positive outlook on life.

Living Authentically: Embracing authenticity means letting go of societal expectations and living in alignment with one's true self, rather than trying to please others.

Real-Life Applications

Passion Finder

- **Prompt:** Make a list of activities or hobbies you loved as a child or teenager. Try one this week and journal about the experience.

- **Example:**

    o   Childhood hobby: Drawing landscapes.

- ○ **Experience:** "I spent an hour drawing today and felt completely absorbed and calm. It reminded me of how much I love expressing myself through art."

Chapter 9: Thriving in a Narcissistic World

In a world where narcissistic behaviors are often glorified, and emotional manipulation is normalized, empaths face an increasingly challenging journey. The social, cultural, and even professional landscapes are frequently permeated with narcissistic attitudes, making it difficult for empaths—individuals who are naturally sensitive to the emotions of others—to navigate relationships and situations without feeling overwhelmed. While living in a narcissistic world can feel exhausting and draining, it's possible to not only survive but to thrive.

This chapter is dedicated to equipping you with the tools and strategies you need to navigate social situations, protect your energy, embrace your empathic gifts, and build a supportive network. By learning how to deal with narcissistic behaviors, protecting your emotional well-being, and building strong, supportive relationships, you can turn your sensitivity into a source of strength and resilience. Let's explore how to thrive in a world that often values narcissism over empathy.

Navigating Social Situations

Navigating social interactions and relationships in a world that is often dominated by narcissistic behaviors requires heightened awareness, emotional intelligence, and clear boundaries. Whether in personal, professional, or public spaces, you may encounter individuals whose behavior is manipulative, self-centered, or emotionally exploitative. Developing strategies for dealing with narcissistic behaviors can help you maintain your sense of self and protect your emotional well-being.

Strategies for Dealing with Narcissistic Behaviors

Empaths are especially vulnerable to narcissistic behavior because of their tendency to absorb the emotions of others and their strong desire to help. Narcissists, on the other hand, can easily manipulate and exploit this empathy to meet their own needs. Knowing how to identify narcissistic traits and developing strategies to protect yourself is essential to thriving in social situations.

1. **Recognizing Narcissistic Traits**

    Narcissists often exhibit a range of behaviors that can be subtle or overt. These behaviors include a lack of empathy, a constant need for validation, a sense of entitlement, and manipulative tactics such as gaslighting, guilt-tripping, or using others for personal gain. Learning to spot these behaviors early can help you protect your emotional energy and avoid being caught in their manipulative web. **Red Flags of Narcissism:**

    o   **Self-Centeredness:** Narcissists often focus conversations solely on themselves and show little genuine interest in others.

    o   **Lack of Empathy:** They may disregard the feelings, needs, and well-being of others.

- o **Gaslighting:** Narcissists frequently distort the truth, making you question your reality and memories.

- o **Entitlement:** They expect special treatment or favor without regard for others.

- o **Chronic Need for Validation:** Narcissists thrive on external admiration and approval, and they will manipulate people to meet these needs.

2. **Pro-Tip:** The first step in navigating narcissistic behavior is recognizing it for what it is. Once you are aware of the signs, you can protect yourself from emotional harm.

3. **Maintaining Emotional Detachment** Narcissists thrive on emotional reactions. They often provoke strong emotions—such as guilt, shame, or anger—in order to maintain control over others. One of the most effective strategies for navigating interactions with narcissistic individuals is emotional detachment. Emotional detachment does not

mean becoming cold or indifferent; rather, it means observing and acknowledging your emotions without allowing them to control your actions or reactions.

Practical Steps:

- o **Observe Without Reacting:** When engaging with a narcissist, try to stay as emotionally neutral as possible. Resist the urge to engage in heated debates or emotional exchanges.

- o **Breathe and Pause:** Take a deep breath before responding to avoid being swept up in an emotional reaction.

- o **Detach from Their Drama:** Narcissists often try to create chaos and drama. Choose to remain calm and unaffected by their antics. This may be difficult at first, but with practice, you can develop emotional resilience.

4. **Setting Boundaries with Narcissists**
Boundaries are essential when interacting with narcissists. These individuals will often test,

challenge, or ignore boundaries to maintain control. Setting and enforcing clear boundaries is crucial for protecting your energy and ensuring that your needs are met. **Boundary-Setting Tips:**

- o **Be Direct and Assertive:** Narcissists respect strength and clear communication. When setting boundaries, be firm and direct. Avoid being wishy-washy or giving in to their demands.

- o **Don't Justify Yourself:** Narcissists may try to argue, manipulate, or guilt-trip you into changing your boundaries. Stand firm and don't feel the need to justify your decisions.

- o **Limit Contact When Necessary:** Sometimes, the best way to set a boundary is to limit or eliminate contact altogether. If the person's behavior is harming your well-being, distance yourself as much as possible.

5. **Avoiding the Trap of People-Pleasing**
Many empaths struggle with people-pleasing tendencies, which make them vulnerable to narcissistic manipulation. Narcissists prey on individuals who are eager to help, fix problems, or avoid conflict. It's important to recognize when you're falling into the trap of people-pleasing and to learn how to say "no" when necessary.

6. **Steps to Overcome People-Pleasing:**

   o **Value Yourself and Your Needs:** Recognize that your needs are just as important as those of others. Practice saying "no" without guilt.

   o **Recognize Manipulative Tactics:** Learn to identify when someone is using guilt or emotional manipulation to get their way. Once you see the tactics, it becomes easier to resist them.

   o **Prioritize Self-Care:** People-pleasing often leads to burnout. Take time to care for yourself—physically, emotionally, and mentally—so that you can be strong and present for others when you choose to.

Protecting Your Energy in Group Settings

Group settings—whether they involve family gatherings, professional meetings, or social events—can be particularly draining for empaths, especially when narcissistic individuals are present. These environments can quickly become toxic if there are narcissists who demand attention or manipulate others for their own benefit. Learning how to protect your energy in group settings is crucial for preserving your mental and emotional well-being.

Energy Protection Techniques

1. **Energetic Grounding**
   Grounding is a powerful practice that helps you stay centered and connected to your own energy. It involves bringing your attention to the present moment and establishing a deep sense of connection with the earth and your

body.

Grounding Practices:

- o **Visualization:** Imagine roots growing from the soles of your feet into the earth, anchoring you securely.

- o **Breathing Techniques:** Take deep, slow breaths and focus on your exhale. This helps release any tension or emotional energy that may be building up.

- o **Mindful Awareness:** Pay attention to your surroundings and sensations, bringing yourself fully into the moment. This prevents you from becoming overwhelmed by external influences.

2. **Energetic Shields and Protection**
Energetic shields are protective barriers you can visualize around yourself to keep negative energy from entering your space. This is especially useful in group settings where narcissists may attempt to draw you into their

drama.

Creating an Energetic Shield:

- o Visualize a bubble or sphere of white light surrounding your body. Imagine it as a protective force field that deflects negative energy.

- o Use this visualization before entering any group setting where you anticipate negative or manipulative behaviors. This shield will help you stay grounded and protected.

3. **Strategic   Self-Placement**

Where you position yourself in a group can significantly affect your energy. Avoid sitting too close to narcissistic individuals, as their presence can drain your emotional reserves.

4. **Tactics for Self-Care in Group Settings:**

- o **Find a Calm Spot:** Choose a position in the room that feels safe and calming. This could be near a window, away from the center of attention, or in a quieter corner.

- o **Take Breaks:** If you start feeling overwhelmed, excuse yourself for a short break. A walk outside or a few moments of silence can help you reset.

5. **Limiting   Interaction**

In large groups, it may be difficult to completely avoid narcissistic individuals. However, you can limit your interaction by being selective about who you engage with and for how long. **Strategies for Limiting Interaction:**

- o **Set Time Limits:** Politely excuse yourself after a set amount of time to avoid being drawn into exhausting conversations or manipulative dynamics.

- o **Redirect Conversations:** If a narcissist tries to dominate the conversation, steer the discussion to neutral topics that aren't likely to escalate into emotional manipulation.

○ **Find Allies:** Seek out other like-minded individuals who share your values and energy. Spending time with supportive people can help balance out the negative energy of narcissists.

Embracing Your Empathic Gifts

While narcissistic behaviors can be toxic, your empathic abilities—your sensitivity to the emotions of others—are not only a gift, but they can also be a source of strength. Learning how to turn your sensitivity into strength is essential for thriving in a narcissistic world.

Turning Sensitivity into Strength

1. **Harnessing Your Emotional Intelligence** Emotional intelligence (EQ) is the ability to recognize, understand, and manage emotions —both your own and others'. For empaths, this means not only understanding and

processing your own feelings but also using your emotional awareness to create meaningful connections and navigate challenging situations.

Building Emotional Intelligence:

- o **Self-Awareness:** Practice regularly tuning into your own emotions and how they affect your thoughts and behaviors. This will help you manage your emotional responses more effectively.

- o **Empathy:** Use your ability to tune into others' feelings in a healthy and constructive way. When you understand others' emotions, you can respond with compassion, not just sympathy.

- o **Emotional Regulation:** Practice self-soothing techniques to maintain emotional balance during stressful or confrontational situations. Deep breathing, meditation, and mindfulness can help you stay calm under pressure.

2. **Setting Boundaries Around Your Empathy**
Your ability to empathize deeply with others is a gift, but it can become overwhelming if not managed properly. It's important to set boundaries around your empathic gifts to prevent emotional exhaustion and burnout.
How to Protect Your Empathy:

- o **Recognize Your Limits:** Pay attention to when you're absorbing too much emotional energy from others. If you feel drained, it's okay to step back and recharge.

- o **Learn to Say No:** You don't have to help everyone, and you certainly don't have to solve everyone's problems. Set limits on how much emotional labor you're willing to invest.

- o **Practice Emotional Detachment:** Learn to detach from other people's emotions without completely shutting them out.

It's possible to be compassionate without absorbing their pain.

3. **Using Empathy to Build Connection and Influence**

When used wisely, your empathic abilities can help you connect with others on a deep and meaningful level. This can make you a powerful influence in both personal and professional contexts.

Strategies for Using Your Empathy:

- o **Active Listening:** Listening without judgment allows you to understand others' emotions and perspectives, which can lead to stronger, more authentic connections.

- o **Validate Others:** Empaths are excellent at validating the feelings of others, which can help build trust and rapport in relationships.

- o **Be a Supportive Presence:** When you sense someone is in need, offer your support and understanding. Your kindness and emotional insight can have a profound positive impact.

Building a Support System

Thriving in a narcissistic world requires connection to people who support, understand, and uplift you. Building a strong support system is essential for healing, growing, and maintaining balance in the face of narcissistic toxicity.

The Value of Community and Trusted Confidants

1. **The Importance of Having a Safe Circle**
   A strong support system is a crucial buffer against the toxicity of narcissistic relationships. Whether it's close friends, family members, or colleagues, the people you surround yourself with can either protect you or contribute to your stress levels.
   Characteristics of a Healthy Support System:

   o **Unconditional Support:** You need people who will accept you for who you are without judgment or manipulation.

- o **Mutual Respect:** A healthy support system is built on reciprocity, where both parties give and receive emotional support.

- o **Emotional Availability:** Your confidants should be emotionally present and available to help you process your feelings and experiences.

2. **Finding Fellow Empaths**
As an empath, it can feel isolating to be surrounded by narcissistic individuals who don't understand or appreciate your sensitivity. Finding fellow empaths who share your experiences and values can create a nurturing environment where you can grow and heal together.

How to Find Fellow Empaths:

- o **Join Online Communities:** Many online forums and support groups cater specifically to empaths and those recovering from narcissistic abuse.

- ○ **Attend Workshops or Retreats:** Look for personal growth workshops, spiritual retreats, or empath-focused events where you can meet like-minded individuals.

- ○ **Seek Out Empathetic People:** You don't have to be an empath yourself to understand and appreciate another's sensitivity. Look for people who are naturally kind, compassionate, and open-hearted.

3. **Building Deep, Meaningful Relationships** A strong support system is based on deep, authentic connections. Focus on quality over quantity when it comes to relationships. Cultivate connections that are grounded in mutual understanding, respect, and empathy. **Nurturing Your Support System:**

- ○ **Invest in Connection:** Take the time to foster meaningful relationships. Show appreciation for your friends and family by offering your support in return.

o **Set Healthy Boundaries with Loved Ones:** Even within your support system, it's important to set boundaries. Ensure that your relationships are mutual and that you don't overextend yourself to the detriment of your own well-being.

Conclusion

Thriving in a narcissistic world is possible, even for empaths. By navigating social situations with awareness, protecting your energy, embracing your empathic gifts, and building a strong support system, you can create a life filled with meaning, fulfillment, and resilience. The strategies shared in this chapter offer a roadmap for thriving in environments that often prioritize narcissism over empathy.

The journey may not always be easy, but with patience, self-compassion, and intentionality, you can not only survive the narcissistic world around you but turn your sensitivity into a powerful tool for connection, growth, and healing. Remember, your empathic abilities are a gift, and when used wisely, they can help you thrive in ways that many others cannot.

Chapter 9 Takeaways

Navigating Social Situations: Empaths can use strategies to deal with narcissistic behaviors in social settings and protect their energy from being drained.

Protecting Your Energy in Group Settings: Recognizing when to withdraw or create emotional distance is crucial for empaths to maintain their well-being in group environments.

Embracing Your Empathic Gifts: Empaths can turn their sensitivity into a strength by using emotional intelligence to navigate relationships and create meaningful connections.

The Benefits of Emotional Intelligence: Developing emotional intelligence enables empaths to understand and manage emotions in themselves and others, fostering healthier, more fulfilling relationships.

Building a Support System: Cultivating a strong community of supportive, like-minded individuals provides emotional safety and encouragement.

Connecting with Fellow Empaths: Finding and building relationships with others who understand and share empathic experiences can offer comfort and validation.

Real-Life Applications

Social Armor

- **Prompt:** Identify three strategies to protect your energy in social settings, such as excusing yourself when overwhelmed. Practice these at your next gathering.

- **Example:**

    o Strategy: "If someone dominates the conversation, I'll politely excuse myself to get a drink or check on something."

- ○ **Reflection:** "At a recent event, I used this tactic when overwhelmed. It helped me recharge and stay present."

Chapter 10: Becoming the Empowered Empath

As an empath, your ability to feel the emotions and energy of others is both a profound gift and, at times, a considerable challenge. Living in a world that often prioritizes ego, manipulation, and emotional self-interest can be overwhelming for an empath. Narcissism, emotional abuse, and toxic dynamics may easily leave you feeling depleted, lost, or disconnected from your own sense of self. However, there is another path—one that allows you to embrace your sensitivity, protect your emotional health, and use your gifts for both personal fulfillment and the benefit of others.

This transformation, from a passive, drained empath to an empowered one, is entirely possible. It requires that you see your emotional depth and intuitive sensitivity as strengths, rather than weaknesses, and learn how to navigate the world from a place of self-respect, inner strength, and clarity. Empowerment doesn't mean denying your true nature as an empath —it means fully owning it and becoming a person who can give without overextending, who can care deeply without losing yourself in the process.

In this chapter, we will explore how to define empowerment for yourself, live with purpose, and continue evolving as an empowered empath. We'll delve deeper into the markers of a successful transformation, offer strategies for using your empathic gifts in positive ways, and explore how to continue on the path of empowerment even as challenges arise.

Defining Empowerment for Yourself

The first step toward becoming an empowered empath is to understand what empowerment truly means for you. Empowerment is a deeply personal journey that doesn't look the same for everyone. It's about reclaiming your power and cultivating a life that aligns with your values, passions, and needs. The more you define empowerment on your terms, the more you will feel a sense of direction and confidence in your life.

What a Fulfilling Life Looks Like for You

Empowerment is the ability to shape your life in a way that honors your emotional, mental, and physical well-being. For an empath, this means being clear about what you need to feel fulfilled, content, and balanced.

- **Living authentically**: For many empaths, the road to empowerment involves shedding the layers of societal expectations, past traumas, and external pressures that may have influenced your sense of self. A fulfilling life means living in alignment with your true values and desires.

- **Emotional Balance**: Empowerment is also about balancing your emotional life. As an empath, you will inevitably feel the emotions of those around you. Learning how to regulate and manage your emotions while navigating the emotional worlds of others is key to achieving fulfillment.

- **Healthy Relationships**: Another essential aspect of a fulfilling life is the quality of your relationships. Empowered empaths attract people who respect, appreciate, and reciprocate the love and energy they give. It's about forming meaningful, nourishing connections, whether romantic, platonic, or familial.

- **Self-Compassion and Inner Peace**: A fulfilling life also involves practicing kindness and compassion towards yourself. It is about learning how to set boundaries, say "no" when necessary, and prioritize your needs without guilt. The more you develop self-compassion, the more empowered you become to live a peaceful and joyful life.

The Markers of a Successful Transformation

A successful transformation from being a reactive empath, easily overwhelmed by others, to an empowered empath, grounded in your inner strength, involves many subtle shifts. These markers of transformation reflect your growth and your ability to live with clarity and confidence.

1. **Self-Knowledge and Self-Awareness**
    One of the first signs of empowerment is a deeper awareness of who you are. As you embark on your journey toward empowerment, you begin to differentiate between your emotions and those of others. You become more conscious of your needs and desires and learn how to express them assertively. This awareness allows you to make choices that support your well-being and fulfillment.

2. **Stronger Boundaries**
    Empowerment is reflected in your ability to establish and maintain strong boundaries. An empowered empath knows when to say "no" and when to protect their energy. You will no longer allow toxic or manipulative people to drain you or take advantage of your empathy. You will learn that it's okay to say no without feeling guilty, and that prioritizing your needs is an act of self-love.

3. **Resilience in the Face of Adversity**
    Life will continue to bring challenges, but as

an empowered empath, you will have the emotional resilience to face them head-on. Instead of becoming overwhelmed by adversity or external criticism, you will find ways to stay grounded and focused on your own healing and growth. Whether it's a difficult situation at work, in a friendship, or a romantic relationship, you will have the emotional tools and inner strength to navigate it without losing your sense of self.

4. **A Sense of Purpose and Direction** Empowered empaths often feel a deep sense of purpose, whether it's in their work, relationships, or personal life. Your sensitivity becomes a tool for meaningful contribution. You understand how your gifts can positively impact others, whether by offering support, teaching, creating, or helping others heal.

5. **Self-Respect and Unshakeable Self-Worth** One of the hallmarks of an empowered empath is an unshakable sense of self-worth. You will no longer seek validation from others because you have internalized the knowledge

that you are enough just as you are. Your self-worth is no longer tied to others' opinions or approval; instead, it's grounded in your own understanding of your intrinsic value.

Living with Purpose

Empowerment is not just about personal growth and well-being; it's also about using your gifts to contribute to the world around you. As an empath, your greatest strength lies in your ability to connect deeply with others and use that emotional insight to create positive change. When you live with purpose, you begin to see your empathic nature as a tool for healing, growth, and inspiration.

Using Your Empathy to Uplift Others

Empaths often feel a deep calling to help others. However, an empowered empath knows how to give in ways that are sustainable and fulfilling. Here are some ways you can use your empathic gifts to uplift others:

- **Emotional Support and Active Listening**: Many people simply need someone who will listen to them, without judgment or interruption. As an empath, your ability to truly listen and validate others' feelings is a powerful way to provide emotional support.

- **Creating Safe Spaces**: Empowered empaths can create safe, nurturing environments where others feel understood and supported. Whether in a personal relationship, a community group, or in professional settings, being a compassionate and understanding presence can help others feel safe to express themselves.

- **Mentorship and Coaching**: Sharing your experiences and wisdom with others who are on their own healing journeys can be deeply rewarding. Whether you choose to become a formal mentor or guide others informally, your empathic understanding can be a beacon for those in need of guidance.

- **Social Advocacy and Service**: Empowered empaths often feel drawn to social causes, whether that's advocating for mental health, social justice, environmental causes, or humanitarian efforts. Using your voice and influence to raise awareness about issues that matter to you can give your life greater meaning.

Becoming a Beacon of Strength and Kindness

Empathy, when combined with strength, has the potential to change the world. As you become more empowered, your presence becomes a source of light and inspiration for others. You radiate a sense of calm and compassion that others naturally gravitate toward. Becoming a beacon of strength and kindness doesn't mean abandoning your own needs or sacrificing your well-being for others. It means offering your energy, love, and support from a place of abundance and resilience.

Ways to Radiate Strength and Kindness:

- **Living by Example**: The greatest way you can inspire others is by living in alignment with your values and demonstrating kindness, compassion, and resilience. You set an example through your actions, showing others that it's possible to be strong and compassionate at the same time.

- **Self-Care as a Foundation**: Your strength comes from the foundation of self-care. By prioritizing your emotional and physical health, you create a stable base from which to offer kindness to others. An empowered empath knows that they can't pour from an empty cup, and self-care is essential for maintaining energy and emotional balance.

- **Compassionate Action**: Empaths who are empowered do not just feel for others—they take action when they see a need. This could be as simple as reaching out to a friend in need or as significant as starting a charity or social initiative. Your empathy inspires you to create tangible positive change in the world.

Continuing the Journey

Empowerment for an empath is not a destination but a continuous journey. You will face new challenges and obstacles as you grow and evolve. The key to continued empowerment is flexibility, adaptability, and a commitment to self-reflection.

Adapting as New Challenges Arise

As you evolve, life will continue to present new challenges. These challenges may test your boundaries, your emotional resilience, and your ability to stay true to yourself. As an empowered empath, you will have the tools to face these challenges with grace and confidence.

- **Emotional Regulation**: One of the most important skills an empowered empath can cultivate is emotional regulation. This involves understanding your emotional triggers and using techniques like deep breathing, mindfulness, or journaling to manage your feelings when they become overwhelming.

- **Learning from Setbacks**: There will be times when you fall back into old patterns or when you face setbacks. Instead of beating yourself up or feeling discouraged, use these experiences as opportunities for growth. Reflect on what you've learned and use that insight to navigate future situations more effectively.

Keeping the Balance Between Giving and Protecting

An empowered empath knows that balance is essential. You can give freely, but you must also know when to protect your energy. This balance is crucial to long-term emotional well-being. Regularly check in with yourself to assess how you're feeling—physically, emotionally, and spiritually. If you feel depleted or overwhelmed, it's important to take a step back and recharge. Self-care, healthy boundaries, and a supportive environment are the pillars that will sustain you as you continue on your journey.

Conclusion

Becoming the empowered empath is an ongoing journey of healing, self-discovery, and growth. It requires redefining your relationship with your sensitivity and learning to navigate a world that can sometimes feel emotionally draining. But by embracing your empathic gifts, setting boundaries, and living with purpose, you can create a life that is not only fulfilling but also a source of strength and inspiration for others.

An empowered empath doesn't just survive—they thrive. They become a beacon of compassion, resilience, and kindness, lighting the way for others to do the same. Your journey may be challenging at times, but every step forward is a step toward greater freedom, joy, and purpose. Continue to trust in your own strength, honor your emotional needs, and embrace the path ahead with courage and compassion.

Chapter 10 Takeaways

Defining Empowerment for Yourself: Empowerment means understanding your true value, setting clear intentions, and living in alignment with your own needs and desires.

What a Fulfilling Life Looks Like for You: A fulfilling life as an empowered empath involves emotional balance, personal growth, and authentic relationships.

Living with Purpose: Empaths can use their empathy to uplift others, becoming sources of strength, kindness, and compassion in their communities.

Becoming a Beacon of Strength and Kindness: Empowered empaths inspire others by demonstrating the power of kindness, resilience, and self-love.

Continuing the Journey: The journey toward empowerment is ongoing, requiring adaptability and a commitment to balance between giving and self-protection.

Keeping the Balance Between Giving and Protecting: Empowered empaths learn to protect their energy, giving to others without overextending themselves or losing their sense of self.

Real-Life Applications

Vision for Empowerment

- **Prompt:** Create a vision board or write a manifesto detailing what an empowered life looks like for you.

- **Example:**

  - Vision board: Includes images of serene landscapes, books, supportive friends, and empowering quotes.

  - **Manifesto:** "I will live authentically, prioritize my well-being, and surround myself with people who respect and uplift me."

www.ingramcontent.com/pod-product-compliance
Lightning Source LLC
Chambersburg PA
CBHW051602250726

48653CB00004BA/1292